If the right-win  Barrett holds onto her seat as long as her late predecessor, Ruth Bader Ginsburg, she will still be hearing cases in 2059. That's nearly four decades of consequential decisionmaking, giving the Court's conservative supermajority the opportunity to reshape nearly all American institutions for generations to come.

As the leading progressive magazine in the country, *The Nation* has reported on and debated the Court's repeated transgressions on public life for more than 150 years. This collection of cutting dispatches presents indispensable perspectives on how we reached our current moment—from the repeal of Roe v. Wade to the hollowing out of labor unions, voter protections, campaign-finance regulations, and beyond—and what it will take to find our way out.

Featuring contributions by Elie Mystal, I. F. Stone, Jamie Raskin, Katha Pollitt, Jedediah Britton-Purdy, Patricia J. Williams, and Charles Warren.

The
Nine Have Spoken

Nation Books

Nation Books is a collaboration between *The Nation* magazine and OR Books.

The Nation was founded by abolitionists in 1865 and still appears quarterly in print and online at thenation.com.

OR Books is a publishing company that embraces progressive change in politics, culture and the way we do business. Find out more at orbooks.com.

Forthcoming in Nation Books

American Carnage

Eleven Federal Workers and the Six Months That Wrecked the U.S. Government
By Sasha Abramsky

The Myth of Red Texas

How Reclaiming Our State's Radical Tradition Can Help Us Beat The Right
By David Griscom

Obsolete

Power, Profit, And The Race For Machine Superintelligence
By Garrison Lovely

The
Nine Have Spoken

The Nation vs. the Supreme Court, 1870 to Today

Edited by

Richard Kreitner

Nation Books

Published in association with OR Books

First printing 2025

The manufacturer's authorised representative in the EU for product
safety is Authorised Rep Compliance Ltd, 71 Lower Baggot Street,
Dublin D02 P593 Ireland (www.arccompliance.com)

Typeset by Lapiz Digital. Printed by BookMobile, USA, and CPI, UK.

paperback ISBN 978-1-68219-647-2 • ebook ISBN 978-1-68219-648-9

Table of Contents

Introduction

It would be difficult to overstate the extent to which the American republic's current set of staggering problems and seemingly intractable crises can and should be blamed on a single institution: the United States Supreme Court.

Other actors, of course, bear responsibility as well: a highly distractible mainstream media, corporate kleptocrats, a generation or two of now-discredited neoconservatives and neoliberals pushing domestic and foreign policy initiatives (the drug war, invading Iraq) that it was clear at the time were unjust and unworkable and indeed have not worked out at all (*oops*).

Yet none of them would have been in a position to see their will so consequentially enacted had they not been empowered by the Supreme Court, which, over the last forty or so years, has green-lighted media consolidation and conglomeration, hollowing out the local and independent journalism on which democracy depends; turned corporations into persons (*abracadabra!*), opening the campaign-finance spigots and flooding the public square with dark money; and—still shocking to contemplate— halted the counting of ballots in a presidential election so as to deliver victory to the candidate preferred by a bare majority of its members, with spiraling effects for America and the world that a quarter-century later have not yet ceased. Not to mention rulings that have hollowed out labor unions; overturned hard-earned protections for the right to vote; and annulled the right to have an abortion it had itself previously recognized as inviolable. Most recently (as of this writing), the Court decided that the president is above and beyond the reach of the law—a decision it is no exaggeration to say demolished in one blow an essential pillar of the constitutional system. It is terrifying to think that the conservative justices on the Court are not yet done with their labors. If she holds on as long as Ruth Bader Ginsburg did, Amy Coney Barrett will still be hearing cases in 2059.

It is both freshly infuriating and strangely comforting, at such a moment, to cast a long look back through the history of the Supreme Court and see just how long the questions and issues raised by the justices' recent interventions have been the subject of conversation and debate. *The Nation* has been airing and reporting on such debates since its founding three months after the end of the Civil War, when it was clear the Court would play a vital role shaping the nation that emerged from the ashes. Covering more than a century and a half, the articles, columns, letters, and editorials included in these pages contain eloquent critiques of the Court's trespasses on democracy, its selective application of supposed constitutional principles, and persistent mockery of the justice's half-hearted pleas that the Court stays out of politics and simply applies the Constitution to the issue is at hand. As more than one contributor points out, the Court often claims to be powerless when it comes to protecting individual liberties but somehow finds justification to act as an almighty sovereign when property rights or corporate interests are at stake.

The heyday of Chief Justice Earl Warren (1953 to 1969) offers a brief exception, an era when *Nation* writers and editors rediscovered along with other liberals the value of an activist court. "Of course, the world cannot be improved by law alone," a contributor noted in 1954, after *Brown v. Board of Education*, "but just as surely it cannot be improved without law." The same magazine that two decades earlier had pushed President Franklin Roosevelt to undertake a thorough overhaul of a hidebound Court now celebrated the "wisdom and restraint of Congress" for defeating such initiatives. The writer of that piece, Maxwell Brandwen, cheered the Warren Court's early decisions in favor of civil liberties as "in harmony with the traditional spirit of our country," evidence of "a sensitive regard for high ethical values." Such praise is understandable in the context of a period when, as Brandwen put it, the justices "upheld and even extended the traditional rights of the individual." What a contrast with our own time, when rights are not being extended but rescinded.

Oddly, the magazine did not take notice at the time of some of the most significant Court decisions of the first few decades of its existence. One searches in vain for a response to *Plessy v. Ferguson*, the 1893 decision that endorsed "separate but equal" public schools and other facilities for Black Americans, or the shameful *Korematsu* ruling (1943) that approved the wartime detention of Japanese Americans. After *Brown v. Board of Education* overturned *Plessy* in 1954, *The Nation* more or less skipped right over the news in order to ask the next question the case necessarily raised: What about racial segregation in the North?

Some of the magazine's best writing on the Court emphasizes the complicated relationship between legal strategy and political activism. Two years before *Brown*, the accomplished lawyer and activist Earl B. Dickerson took to *The Nation* to urge his fellow Black Americans to "place less reliance on the goodwill of a few appointed justices" and to focus more on building "strength in the political arena." An editorial about the Court's ruling in *Roe v. Wade* (1973) asked:

> What are the prerequisites for such a reversal of attitude at the highest judicial level? For one thing, there must be a special constituency, imbued with zeal, equipped with reason, and pushing hard for a change in the law. Without an activist vanguard, ancient concepts will not be questioned, much less critically examined.

Tragically, the right, not the left, got the message, at least regarding reproductive rights. It's poignant and depressing to read several decades' worth of warnings in *The Nation* that, thanks to the anti-abortion "activist vanguard" channeling political organizing into federal judicial appointments, *Roe* would soon be on the chopping block. It only took forty-nine years, but with the *Dobbs* decision of 2022, the "special constituency" accomplished their goal at last.

The pages that follow contain repeated and consistent warnings that readers should not get too hopeful about the possibilities of liberation via court decree, nor place too much trust in a fundamentally undemocratic institution. "Not a few timid liberals still fear curtailment of the court's swollen powers lest it be unable to protect us from fascism," the young I.F. Stone (still Isidor Feinstein) wrote in 1937, at the height of the battle over Roosevelt's "court-packing" plan. "This is pure fancy."

Trump v. United States (2024), which is where this book ends, offers more conclusive proof than Stone could ever have hoped—or feared—to be able to marshal in support of his case. "Far from being a bulwark against fascism," Stone presciently wrote, "the court may serve a double function in its rise. If the court continues to hamstring Congress and state legislatures, it will play directly into the hands of the fascist demagogue who sneers at the 'inefficiency' of democratic processes. On the other hand, a fascist regime will find material in past court decisions to provide itself with legal, nay, 'constitutional,' justification." What could be more useful to such a regime than the Court's approval of the idea once put forward by Richard Nixon, to the howls of a horrified nation, that the president is forever shielded from prosecution for crimes committed while in office?

To informed and thoughtful left-leaning Americans, it has never not seemed cruel and absurd for so much of our lives to be determined by nine berobed attorneys granted effectively insuperable authority and, with life tenure, immunized against the discontent of the governed. All the more so these days, when several of the justices are known in their private lives to possess little personal integrity and to align with insurrectionists against the government they are sworn to serve.

From I.F Stone and other early *Nation* writers' demands for Court reform to justice correspondent Elie Mystal's impassioned and astute coverage in recent years, this collection of

Nation writings about the Court puts the choices we face today in proper historical perspective. It shows that the justices' recent spate of reactionary rulings is not a departure from history but a return to the norm, and that proposing ideas for overhauling the Court should not be considered particularly radical or beyond the pale. Rather, questioning the Court's legitimacy, demanding a more democratic, accountable federal judiciary, is a tradition nearly as old as the Court itself.

Richard Kreitner
September 2024

Note: Some of the pieces here, especially the older ones, have been edited for length. Any words that have been added for clarification are marked in brackets.

PART ONE

Rethinking The Court

The Burden of the Supreme Court

January 13, 1870

To the editor of *The Nation*:

Speaking on behalf of the Federal judiciary, I earnestly appeal to the editor of the *Nation*, and to all thoughtful men who desire to preserve the moral power of the judiciary and the law-revering character of our people, to assist in taking from the judicial branch of the Government a burden which it is the least able to bear, freeing it at the same time from the popular clamor and odium which is flung at it whenever an unpopular constitutional decision is rendered by a divided court, and at the same time bringing the responsibility of guarding the Constitution home to the legislative branch, where it properly belongs. This responsibility is dragging down the judiciary.

It is undeniable that the most important constitutional decisions have come to us from a divided court, and that the views of the judges have generally gone according to their former political opinions; so that the public have often been able to predict the decision before it was announced; while the judicial opinions within the Court have been little else than a reflex of the political opinions without. It may also happen that a statute which has been passed by large majorities in the two Houses of Congress, and which has been maturely considered and deliberately approved by the President, examined, moreover, by the Attorney-General, and sanctioned by all of the President's constitutional advisers, and, finally, which is pronounced constitutional by four judges of the Supreme Court, may be absolutely annulled, and declared not to exist, by five. When this divided Court and bare majority move counter to the general public sentiment of the day, the general public sentiment of the day seizes on the opinions of the four dissenting members as conclusively right, pronounces the five controlling members prejudiced, dishonest, and, perhaps, corrupt, and thinks the Supreme Court, and, mayhap, the Constitution itself, a nuisance used to thwart the people in making their own laws.

Furthermore, the members of the Supreme Court, holding for life, and changing at rare intervals, must, in the nature of things, hold to the public sentiment of the past rather than the public sentiment of the day. It is not wonderful, therefore, that there have been these jarrings of opinions; and so long as the public sentiment travels rapidly and the judicial sentiment slowly, such jarrings may be expected and will be inevitable.

It remains, then, for thoughtful men to think of a remedy. Perhaps [Illinois senator Lyman] Trumbull's plan, requiring a concurrence of two-thirds of the Supreme Court to declare a law unconstitutional, is a step in the right direction. Yet, so long as part of a court uphold a law as constitutional, and its validity or annulment depends on the accident of judicial changes or on the political training of the majority, will it not be more logical and rational to require a concurrence of all the judges? When an act of Congress is so clearly void that no member of the Supreme

Court pronounces it valid, and the judicial mind of the Court as a unit stamps it as a legislative inadvertence, then the decisions of the Court will be restored in public estimation to their former majesty.

A MEMBER OF THE FEDERAL JUDICIARY

Washington, January, 1870

Reforming the Supreme Court

Raymond Leslie Buell
June 14, 1922

Nearly a hundred years ago Alexis de Tocqueville said that the power of the American Supreme Court was "the power of public opinion," but that it would last only "as long as the people respect the law," and that it "would be impotent against popular neglect or contempt of the law." This is a double-edged warning—applying equally to Judges and to people—which has lost none of its timeliness with the passing of years. And it should not be presumptuous to reiterate it in the face of recent decisions of the Supreme Court which strike directly at social legislation the necessity for which is almost universally recognized.

During the present term the court has overruled an Arizona law forbidding the use of an injunction in labor disputes, on the ground that such an enactment deprived the employer of his rights without due process of law. Many years ago the court ruled that the right of indictment by grand jury, the right not to testify against oneself, and even the right to a jury trial might be taken away by a State without violating the due process clause of the Fourteenth Amendment. If the anti-injunction provision of the Arizona law is unconstitutional, a similar provision in the Clayton Act [1914]—widely heralded as Labor's

Magna Carta—would logically be unconstitutional, because of the due-process clause in the Fifth Amendment, applying to acts of Congress.

Regardless of the logic used by the court to reconcile its decisions of the present with those of the past, it is high time that the actual extent of its powers be reexamined. The Supreme Court now has the power to survey every act of Congress to determine whether or not it conflicts with the Constitution of the United States. It has the power, under the Fourteenth Amendment as interpreted by a long line of decisions, to survey every act of the Forty-eight State legislatures within the Union in order to determine whether they deprive persons of life, liberty, or property without due process of law. There was a time when the Supreme Court inquired merely into the *power* to enact the legislation in question. The court still insists that it follows this rule. Nevertheless, under the Fourteenth Amendment the court has come to pass upon the *expediency* of State legislation under the famous "Rule of Reason" whereby it determines whether or not the act of the State is reasonable. A test of reasonableness inevitably becomes a test of expediency rather than of power. In applying this test the court has practically deserted its position as a Judicial body and has become a third chamber in every State legislature in the country. It serves as the same check to legislative majorities as does the British House of Lords.

Naturally, a body possessed of such power subjects itself to attack. Even before 1800, the Georgia House passed a bill which provided that any Federal marshal who attempted to carry out the judgment of the Supreme Court in *Chisholm v. Georgia* "shall be guilty of felony, and shall suffer death, without benefit of clergy, by being hanged." Later decisions aroused less violent protests. Nevertheless, both Presidents Jackson and Lincoln failed to carry out the mandates of the Federal courts. And after the Civil War, the sentiment of Congress against the Supreme Court because of its treatment of reconstruction measures was so great that bills were introduced abolishing the appellate jurisdiction of the court altogether.

At present, there is only one direct means of controlling the decisions of the Supreme Court: that is by impeachment. Its judges hold office for good behavior and its decisions cannot be overcome. Yet, obviously, impeachment is no remedy. A judge cannot be impeached for a decision made in good faith, however distasteful it may be.

Many drastic suggestions have been made to curtail this vast authority of the Federal judiciary. It has been pointed out that the Constitution in no place expressly grants the power to declare laws unconstitutional and that this power is exercised by the courts in few, if any, of the other governments of the world. On the ground of "usurpation," there are those who would wipe out entirely the power of judicial review. Yet, there are at least three reasons why such a heroic remedy would be a mistake. Practically, it would necessitate a constitutional amendment because the courts would undoubtedly decide that this right was inherent in the nature of judicial power and that, to quote the *Federalist*, it followed "from the general theory of a limited Constitution." Secondly, it would allow Congress to encroach without restraint upon the powers of the State and thus make possible the destruction of the federal nature of the Union. Of more immediate importance, it would give rise to forty-eight different constructions of Federal laws by State courts beyond which there would be no appeal; and it would allow State legislatures to pass laws violating the Federal Constitution. In all federalisms, the power exists in the federal government to declare the legislation of smaller units unconstitutional. The abolition of this power in the United States would, finally, remove a desirable check on the domination of Congress by special interests, whether they be Agricultural blocs, American Legions, or Anti-Saloon Leagues. And it would deprive the country of the services of the one branch of our Government where learning and intellect are conspicuous.

Realizing that the general principle of judicial review is sound, others have advocated the popular election of judges in order to keep them in closer contact with public opinion. But the popular election of judges in the States has, if anything, reduced the character of State judiciaries. It is impossible for an electorate, especially when nation-wide, to pass upon judicial qualities. Such a reform would drag the court into politics more than ever. Likewise, President [Theodore] Roosevelt's idea of the recall of judicial decisions—whereby the people would vote on questionable decisions—contradicts every idea of judicial power. It is subject to the same objection as the popular election of judges. It would be impossible to have the whole nation vote on the constitutionality of a State law invalidated by the Supreme Court. The American Federation of Labor has suggested that the power of the court to pass on the constitutionality of State legislation should be retained but that its power to supervise acts of Congress should be taken away. But this change would also place the protection of federalism and private rights in the hands of Congress, and if no other changes were made, it would leave uncontrolled the power of the court to overrule State laws which may be the result of a widespread demand.

The most reasonable method of controlling the power of judicial review would be to require unanimity or at least a two-thirds majority before the court could set a law aside on the ground of unconstitutionality. The practical advantage of this change is that it would probably not require the tedious enactment of a constitutional amendment. Congress already possesses the power to regulate the number of judges on the court, to fix their salaries, and to make "such exceptions" and "such regulations" in the appellate jurisdiction of the court as it wishes. Practically all cases involving constitutionality come before the court on appeal. A law regulating the manner of these appeals would seem to fall within the power of Congress, especially since the actual exercise of judicial review by the court would be retained.

In 1911, Great Britain passed a Parliament Act which took away from the House of Lords its absolute veto of bills passed by the Commons, but which left it the right to suspend ordinary legislation passed by the lower house for at least two years. The Supreme Court of the United States is not a hereditary body; it does not represent privilege. Nevertheless, it exercises much the same power as the House of Lords, and it is just as likely to lose touch with public opinion because of the cloistered life in which it is sheltered and because of the conservatism which constant contact with musty legal precedents inevitably gives.

Shall We Remake the Supreme Court?

Charles Warren
May 7, 1924

Recent decisions by the Supreme Court of the United States, holding that Congress has exceeded its authority in passing legislation not warranted by the Constitution, have revived the discussion as to the exercise by the courts of the power of judicial review. It is urged by some that this power to pass upon the validity of acts of Congress, even assuming its legality, should be abolished or limited. By others, the lawful existence of the power is absolutely denied; its exercise is said to be a "usurpation"; it is claimed that Congress is the final judge of its right to legislate on any subject; and it is pointed out (apparently under the mistaken notion that English practice would be applicable here) that in England and in most European countries, the Parliament is the supreme judge of its own powers.

There is a very necessary reason, however, why in the United States Congress should not be its own final arbiter. Unlike England, the United States has a federal form of government, under which, in the same territory and over the same body of citizens, two distinct governments operate—the National and the State—each limited in its powers by the provisions of the Constitution. One of the most important classes of questions which come before the Supreme Court, therefore, is that in which the claim is advanced by one or the other of the parties to the suit that either Congress or the State legislature has exceeded these limited powers. No such question can come before an English court with respect to acts of Parliament, since no such class of limitations on the powers of Parliament exists.

If the United States possessed no Supreme Court, with authority to say when Congress or a State legislature had trespassed beyond the field assigned to them respectively by the Constitution, then both Congress and the State legislatures would have full power to legislate at their own sweet will, utterly unrestricted by the provisions of the Constitution. And, as a natural and inevitable consequence, Congress, being the mightier body, would prevail in every instance, and national legislation might sweep away all boundaries between the nation and the States in any case in which Congress felt sufficiently strongly the necessity or desirability of so doing. As to the citizens of the States, Congress might violate every one of the Bill of Rights contained in the first ten amendments, and no citizen of a State would have any redress in court. Of the later amendments, each might be violated at will by Congress, if unrestricted by the judiciary; and Congress might, therefore, authorize the sale of intoxicating liquors, in complete violation of the Eighteenth Amendment, or it might directly legislate as to the rights of Negroes in the States, in violation of the Fourteenth Amendment.

In other words, instead of a federal government with limited powers, and with complete reservation to the States and their citizens of all other powers and rights, we should have a consolidated government with unlimited powers, and with no rights left to the States and their citizens except such as Congress, in its supreme autocracy, might see fit to leave or to grant to them. That this is no imaginary danger is shown by the fact that Congress has, in the past, enacted at least ten laws violating the Bill of Rights; and the citizens have been protected only because the court has held that the Constitution must prevail in their defense over such laws of Congress.

The voters of this country, if they so desire, have the right, of course, at any time to change the powers and functions of the branches of their government, provided they do it in the method required by the Constitution, i.e., by amendments duly adopted by the necessary votes of Congress and of the States. But when such a change is suggested as the destruction of the most important function of the Supreme Court, the voters ought to be made to realize, in advance, that this change means the destruction of their federal form of government.

If the Supreme Court Objects

Paul Y. Anderson
July 19, 1933

It is often and pertinently asked what the United States Supreme Court will say about the constitutionality of some of the Roosevelt measures. Certainly there are at least three reactionary old men on that bench who would take profound satisfaction in standing by their plutocratic concepts of society even if they knew the mob was battering at the door, and there may be more than three. That eventuality already has been seriously considered here by persons interested in the success of the New Deal. There are ways of meeting it. Congress could pass an act requiring members of the court to retire upon reaching a certain age. That would remove two of the worst. It would also remove the best, Justice Brandeis, but that could be met by a provision enabling the President by executive order to extend the tenure of designated Justices who had reached the age limit. Or the size of the court could be increased by law to permit the appointment of additional Justices whose ideas developed subsequent to the year 1880. It has been done. If this reporter knows anything about the temper of the present Administration, it will never permit the whole economic structure of this country to be disrupted and demoralized because fewer than half a dozen dyspeptic old men are determined to uphold precedents established before the invention of the telephone. As has often been made clear in these pages, I do not relish these encroachments of the executive upon the prerogatives of the other branches, but sometimes a condition arises which must be dealt with. The blame for such bad precedents properly rests on those who produce the conditions.

Fallacies About the Court

Morris R. Cohen
July 10, 1935

That the people of the United States favor the NRA [National Recovery Administration] was made obvious by the unprecedented Congressional majority accorded to the Administration in the election of 1934. What, then, prevents Congress from passing a bill enlarging the Supreme Court with ten additional judges who, on a rehearing, are sure to vote for the constitutionality of the original act?

There is a general impression that this would be dishonest. Why so? Because, according to the traditional assumption, judges have nothing to do with making the law, their decisions following with logical necessity from "the solemn will of the people expressed in the Constitution," and if the results are bad, we should go through the laborious ordeal of changing the Constitution rather than the composition of the court. This view has so often been repeated that it is generally accepted as axiomatic. Nevertheless, it rests on a number of rather obvious fallacies.

1) That the judges merely find the meaning of the Constitution and in no way make or mold it has long been characterized among scientific jurists as a childish fiction. No one can seriously maintain

that all of our constitutional law as to what constitutes interstate commerce, the police power of the states, or due process of law follows logically from the wording of the Constitution and has not been affected by the social, economic, and political opinions of different judges. The law took a different direction under Taney than under Marshall. Indeed, how could the people in 1789—or the small proportion of them who had the right to vote then— have foreseen all the modern inventions and made definite provisions for them? It is certainly not through anything written in the Constitution that the power to regulate interstate commerce includes the power to prohibit the sending of liquor into certain states but not the power to regulate insurance. A thousand similar distinctions may be mentioned which, whether justified or not by their practical consequences, are certainly judge-made and might have been different if other judges had ruled.

Specifically, the NRA is declared unconstitutional because it delegates legislative power to the President. But the fact is that all effective legislation for the future must inevitably delegate some subsidiary lawmaking to the executive authority. The line between proper and improper delegation is not laid down in the Constitution itself. Where to draw it is a question of political wisdom. Why should the courts rather than Congress determine it? The usual answer is that the Constitution declares itself to be the supreme law of the land, and its interpretation must therefore be left to the courts. This, however, cannot be consistently maintained. The Constitution provides that every state shall be guaranteed a republican form of government. What does that mean? There are, in fact, many express provisions of the Constitution which the courts cannot or dare not enforce.

The truth, then, is that constitutional law is just what judges make it. A leading conservative newspaper put it aptly when it said that the United States Supreme Court is a continuous constitutional convention. This it is in fact. But we do not generally recognize it, else we should demand that the work of this constitutional convention be ratified by the people before it goes into effect, or at any rate that the delegates be more responsive to, and in closer touch with, popular needs.

2) We are frequently told that the Constitution represents the eternal principles of justice, or at least those principles of liberty and right which are characteristic of Anglo-Saxon civilization. The first of these claims is obviously question-begging; specific decisions which strike people as unjust can certainly not be defended that way. The second claim is even more readily disposed of by the fact that our English cousins have never given their courts power to set aside legislation on grounds of unconstitutionality.

3) Quite fallacious also is the rhetorical argument that without this power vested in the courts we should be at the mercy of legislative majorities. This argument ignores the historic fact that in few, if any, actual cases have the majority of our people felt themselves saved from Congressional oppression by judicial intervention. On the contrary, Congress being more responsive to popular demand, our people as a whole have felt more resentment at being at the mercy of small judicial majorities than at being at the mercy of very large legislative majorities. Besides, the mischief of Congressional wrongs can be readily remedied at the next election, while the mischief of wrong judicial decisions

in the name of the Constitution requires the laborious consent of two-thirds of each house of Congress and three-quarters of the state legislatures.

If we need watchers to protect us from bad legislation, why not watchers against bad judicial decisions? The fact is that the people of England, France, Switzerland, or the Scandinavian countries feel as free as we do, and their rights are as amply protected, without their courts having the power to set aside legislation as unconstitutional.

4) It is quite fallacious to argue that our system assures a maximum security of legal rights and thus encourages business enterprise. The actuality is rather the other way. In no other civilized country would people endure a legal system in which such a question as that of the legality of certain codes could remain undetermined for two years. In no other country also is there such a complete separation between power and responsibility as in ours, where those who have the final word on all questions of law are in no way answerable to the popular will or to any other earthly authority.

5) It is generally urged that the judicial veto over legislation has been in force since the case of *Marbury v. Madison* in 1803, and it is too late to change it. This argument is historically untenable. What that famous case did decide was that the court would not issue a mandamus to compel a Democratic Secretary of State to deliver certain commissions to some Federalists, even though an act of Congress authorized it to do so. The actual decision was a quite satisfactory victory for the Democratic Administration and not something over which the country got excited. In his

written opinion, Marshall did, in the fashion of his day, indulge in speculations about constitutions written for all time and superior to acts of Congress; but most of it was mere dictum. From the chaos which would follow a consistent adherence to the theory of three independent departments of the government, we have been saved by the process of practical accommodation and the extra-legal party system.

The first case in which the Supreme Court exercised the right to set aside a law of general importance was the *Dred Scott* case, and the decision and the dicta in that case were repealed by force of arms. It is only in recent times that declaring acts of Congress unconstitutional may be said to have become a practice.

6) The subordination of Congress to the courts has often been defended on the ground that under this system we have greatly prospered. This is a rather naive example of the fallacy of *post hoc ergo propter hoc.* Our prosperity, if it is a fact, may be due to our unrivaled natural resources, to the practical skill of our people, and the like. And it may well be argued that our present depression is in part due to such judicial vetoes as those of the Lochner case, the Adair case, the child-labor cases, the minimum-wage cases, and others, which by depressing the economic power of the laboring classes have depressed our home markets.

7) When we realize that the important questions which come before our highest court involve political, economic, and technical issues, then if we lay aside pious rhetoric, we must admit that far from being the strongest, the judiciary is the weakest part of our governmental system—for it has the least opportunity of getting adequate information. No one who wants to inform

himself thoroughly on any question will be satisfied to do so on the basis of listening for a few hours to two lawyers who have submitted argumentative briefs.

8) Space does not permit discussion of the relation of our federal courts to state legislation. But if the virtue of a federal system be the opportunity for different experiments in different states, that virtue has been effectively minimized by the way in which the Supreme Court has turned the Fourteenth Amendment— intended by the people as a protection for the Negroes—into a prohibition of experiments in the field of social legislation.

The Supreme Court and Civil Liberties

Isidor Feinstein (I.F. Stone)
February 6, 1937

This year, we celebrate the 150th anniversary of the signing of the Constitution. The Bill of Rights will feature in after-dinner speeches, and newspapers will repeat the noble phrases that have come from the Supreme Court in defense of civil liberties. Few will mention that these phrases come almost entirely from dissenting opinions and that the Bill of Rights—under the expert manipulation of the federal courts—has never been what it was thought to be. The Constitution is 150 years old, but the decision in *De Jonge vs. Oregon*, handed down on January 4, happens to be the first in all that time in which the constitutional guarantee of free speech, press, and assembly was applied by the Supreme Court in a case involving a radical. That the court has always—or almost always—been ready to defend the liberties of conservatives will remain of merely academic importance until police begin beating up members of the Union League for criticizing the government. A decision setting aside the conviction of a Communist, De Jonge, under the Oregon criminal-syndicalism law is genuinely a victory for civil liberties.

Even this victory may be overestimated. De Jonge was arrested at a meeting called by the Communist Party in Portland, Oregon, to protest against the illegal raids made by the police in their effort to break the longshoremen's strike in 1934. He was sentenced to seven years in jail for "criminal syndicalism." Despite the capacity of the judicial mind to befog the simplest issue when fog is advantageous, De Jonge's conviction could hardly be regarded as other than a clever invasion of fundamental liberties. It is indicative of how far we have drifted that we are so pleasantly surprised when the court begins to recognize the obvious.

The De Jonge decision may even have drawbacks. Liberal decisions have often been won in the past at the expense of establishing restrictive principles that bear evil fruit in later cases. The Supreme Court in this case decided only that no man could be found guilty of criminal syndicalism merely for participating in a meeting held under Communist auspices. The court goes on to tell what offenses De Jonge might have been convicted of: " ... while the defendant was a member of the Communist Party, he was not indicted for participating in its organization, or for joining it, or for soliciting members, or for distributing its literature." De Jonge's case was "remanded for further proceedings not inconsistent with this opinion." Do these words mean that if De Jonge were now to be indicted and convicted of joining the Communist Party, or recruiting members for it, or distributing its literature, the court would be ready to uphold the conviction? Has the court laid the basis for greater restrictions than ever on civil liberties under our state criminal-syndicalism and anarchy laws?

Past experience underscores the necessity for vigilance. The Bill of Rights is prominent in the official portrait of the court, but plays an inglorious role in its actual history. The federal courts were enthusiastic in their enforcement of the Sedition Act under Adams. The Supreme Court was ineffective in its one puny gesture of protest against Lincoln's suspension of habeas corpus, and with it of all basic rights, during the Civil War. The court helped to forge new instruments of repression in its interpretation of the immigration laws. It was ready to find excuse in far-fetched analogies for the use and abuse of the Espionage Act during the World War. It has consistently upheld criminal-syndicalism laws, products of the post-war red scares. The De Jonge case and its predecessors disclose the wide gap between myth and fact even in a civilized community. Our legal soothsayers have succeeded in portraying as a tribune of the people a governmental organ whose most consistent and con-spicuous function has been the adaptation of our basic law to the needs of corporate enterprise. Not a few timid liberals still fear curtailment of the court's swollen powers lest it be unable to protect us from fascism. This is pure fancy.

No construction has been too broad when property rights were before the court. It has been ready to enlarge on the Constitution and to invoke the divine order of things to legalize some of the greatest steals in our history. But it looked the other way when the Chicago anarchists were hung, Debs was jailed, and Sacco and Vanzetti sent to the chair. It will cut through all proce-dural difficulties and overturn well-established precedents to review both law and fact when a utility company appeals from a rate-cut order, but it falls back on extremes of legal punctilio when human lives and basic liberties are at stake, especially those of radicals—that is, of those who most need protection. Far from being a bulwark against fascism, the court may serve a double function in its rise. If the court continues to hamstring Congress and state legislatures, it will play directly into the hands of the fascist demagogue who sneers at the "inefficiency" of democratic processes. On the other hand, a fascist regime will find material in past court decisions to provide itself with legal, nay, "constitutional," justification.

A United Front on the Court

K.N. Llewellyn
March 14, 1937

The Supreme Court issue has reached the stage where an anti-tory united front becomes necessary, moving along the only line which is immediately practicable, to wit, the President's program. It is lamentable that this should have become necessary. The President's program is unfortunate from every angle but one; it is much as if a man who needed transportation should mortgage his future for four times the price of a good car, to buy a buggy and an elephant. The choice has become, however, one between the elephant-and-buggy or no transportation at all.

The underlying issue is clear. It is not age or pressure of business. It is the attitude of justices toward allowing the government to attempt desperately needed social and economic readjustments, partly known, in greater part as yet unforeseen.

Now the Supreme Court has become, and is, the embodiment and oracle of the Constitution. What seems to escape many liberals, especially liberal constitutional lawyers, is that the court will continue to be such embodiment and oracle despite most considerable overhauling. The court's position is not dependent upon matters which—like this one—are tiny in relation to its great tradition and function. Let us not lose perspective. The idea and ideal of the Constitution are of tremendous value to our national life. An idea and an ideal need embodiment to remain effective; but the embodiment takes on much of the sanctity of the ideal. Moreover, the court has, over the long haul, given great and statesmanlike service. Even in the more recent unfortunate decisions, its veto has forced the drafting of better and more adequate legislation.

But the court has persistently and continuously overstepped that reasonable leeway to go wrong which any oracle requires if it is to be wise. The present is again a time of need and crisis. We need action. But the majority of the court have given sign that they do not propose to let us have the action which we need, or even a reasonable part of it, or even to experiment toward salvation. Primitive peoples, in such conditions, get rid of the priest or the oracle. When rain fails persistently, they act.

The President proposes nothing so drastic. He proposes only putting enough new blood into our college of priests to overcome the inertia of the more frozen members. It is fairly to be expected that this will, for the moment, get results. Such results will come at an embarrassing cost. I do not indeed feel that the move will really shake the authority of the court among any persons who would not have had their respect shaken equally by a mere shift in the present alignment of the justices. For the Supreme Court is hardy as a mountain cedar; it has maintained its high position through worse storms than this, despite the prophets of calamity then and now.

What is unfortunate is the fact that as a bench increases in size, its capacity to do the work of a bench—really to consult and

advise together, instead of making speeches at one another—
rapidly decreases. Seven would today be a more effective working team than nine. It is not to be forgotten that the court carries
a huge load of business, business worth doing well, which never
gets into the public prints at all. That load will be worse handled, much worse, by fifteen. Nor is it to be forgotten that mere
approval of legislation is not the task even of a liberal majority.
They have before them a necessary and terrific labor, of overhauling our whole theory of constitutional law. Leave that task
undone or badly done, and our children will inherit trouble. It
is a task which calls for sustained and coherent group-thinking
hard to work out in any bench of many members.

It troubles me less that the President's proposed action
amounts to "meddling with the court." This court and others have been meddled with again and again, without losing
their independence. Life tenure alone gives a fair assurance on
that point; let alone the well-known misjudgments of recent
Presidents about their appointees; or, say, the history of New
York's successive remodeling of its highest court. The most
troublesome thought is that, this one measure accomplished,
the reform movement may die down. We need, beyond the
President's proposal, provision for a two-thirds' vote, at least,
to wipe out an act of the two constitutionally coordinate
powers. We need also an amendment expressly and unequivocally enlarging the powers of Congress—preferably under the
general-welfare clause. To have such more permanent measures as these choked off by the President's proposed poulticing
of the existent evil would be tragic.

But the issue has been drawn. It has been inescapably drawn. It is not pleasant for one interested in adequate legal engineering to be forced into "Yes" or "No" on such a costly, inept, and equivocal line of engineering as the President has proposed. But issues are drawn by the powers that be. We cannot redraw them. The lesser evil lies unmistakably in supporting the President in this proposal. In supporting him—and actively. In setting up a counter-barrage of opinion and of pressure. In keeping up and increasing that counter-barrage. To be inert is to be overridden—and ridden over. We need a united front.

PART TWO

The Warren Court

Negro Rights and the Supreme Court

Earl B. Dickerson
July 12, 1952

The tide of New Deal liberalism reached its crest in Congress and the White House in the late 1930s. In the Supreme Court, the crest came in the first year or two of the next decade. The court in which Justices Black, Douglas, Murphy, and Rutledge joined forces was the one that most widely extended the constitutional safeguards of the right to picket, to distribute leaflets, to hold public meetings, and to express unpopular views. Between the years 1937 and 1945, the court gave the Bill of Rights new breadth and depth and came close to restoring to the freedoms of the First Amendment the spirit and meaning the Founding Fathers intended it to have.

The decline of the New Deal ended the era of liberalism. The Cold War and the rapid development of a war psychology sent the Bill of Rights into a tailspin. Decision after decision has imposed limitations on the very civil rights which before 1945 the court had protected and extended. Loyalty oaths have been given the stamp of judicial approval. Men have been imprisoned for the crime of conspiring to "teach" and "advocate." Lawfully resident aliens have been held deportable for their espousal of unorthodox political views even if they had renounced those views before passage of the laws under which their deportation was ordered. Dissemination of opinions by the use of sound trucks—an important medium of communication to minority groups now that most mass-communication media are in the hands of the wealthy—is frowned upon where once it was protected. When the police have considered a speech potentially provocative of violence, they have been upheld by the court in their attempt to preserve order by silencing the speaker instead of by controlling the violence.

All these developments in Supreme Court doctrine restrict the right of protest against the status quo, effectively deterring the unpopular, the oppressed, the minority from speaking up in favor of change. For Negro citizens, who as the major victims of discrimination have the most vital interest in preserving the broadest freedom to protest, they carry a special threat. In an atmosphere of restraint of free speech, only individuals of great courage will speak out vigorously against Jim Crow laws, poll-tax restrictions, and failure to prosecute those who take part in mob violence against Negroes. In short, the attitude of the court casts a shadow of fear even over areas which its decisions do not literally cover.

Paradoxically, however, the same court which has thus emasculated the Bill of Rights has also denied injunctive enforcement of the restrictive covenant. And it has refused to allow the states totally to exclude Negroes from the benefits of higher education made available to other races. Unfortunately, the undeniable progress reflected by these decisions creates the danger that Negroes may look to the court to save them from the evils of an era of repression. That they would find its decisions a slender reed to lean on is apparent from the record.

After the "emancipation" which Negroes thought they had gained from the Civil War, the court soon found formulas for keeping them "in their place." In 1875, the *Cruikshank* decision construed the civil rights legislation of the Reconstruction era so restrictively that it was rendered almost meaningless. In 1883, the decision that the Fourteenth Amendment applied only to action by the state and not to action by individuals made the Negro fair prey to a host of discriminations which plague him to this day. And soon the court evolved a mechanism for permitting state governments to discriminate. In 1896, in *Plessy v. Ferguson*, it enunciated the "separate but equal" doctrine, allowing segregation so long as the separated races were given "equal" treatment. The struggle against discrimination which Negroes have carried on in the courts for the past fifty-six years has been largely a struggle to erase *Plessy* from the statute books. Having been allowed to survive for fifty-six years, this doctrine has spawned a multitude of laws in the Southern states compelling segregation in schools, libraries, railroad facilities, hospitals, theaters, playgrounds, beaches, restaurants, penal institutions, welfare institutions, voting places, and even telephone booths and lavatories.

*

Clearly, the court must be made to see what is becoming increasingly evident to the American people—that the promise of equal justice for all will remain a fiction as long as segregation is tolerated. And as long as Negroes can obtain only unequal justice, the Fourteenth Amendment is deprived of a large part of its intended substance as a guarantor of the rights of national citizenship.

Another challenge to the court to strike Plessy down is presented by two cases awaiting argument in the fall—one from Clarendon County, South Carolina, and one from Kansas [*Brown v. Board of Education*]. The issue in both is elementary-school segregation, and it will be interesting to see whether a majority of the justices will be able to devise a new technique for perpetuating the segregation pattern.

Many Negro leaders believe that the position of the Supreme Court will be determined by the growing political significance of the Negro, both nationally and internationally. On the domestic scene, the Negro vote may be decisive in Northern urban centers and is potentially a factor to be considered in some areas of the South. On the international scene, American injustice to the Negro has propaganda value for the Kremlin and must therefore be condemned. The Negro is compelled to recognize that he can place less reliance on the goodwill of a few appointed justices than on his strength in the political arena. For the development of that strength, he must have freedom to organize and freedom to voice his discontents.

The Negro cannot afford, therefore, to isolate his fight for his people's rights from the broader struggle to preserve the protections of the Bill of Rights. He cannot afford to limit his demands to anti-poll-tax measures, anti-lynch laws, and the abolition of segregation, but must join, for his own interest, in the fight for repeal of the Smith act, the McCarran act, and the Taft-Hartley act. Only when there has been created an atmosphere of political liberalism in which men cannot be imprisoned for their political views will the overturn of the *Plessy v. Ferguson* decision become inevitable.

Nine Men Speak To You

Fredric Wertham
June 12, 1954

At a time when the attention of the whole country was focused on the Army-McCarthy hearings, an epoch-making event took place. The United States Supreme Court decided that segregation of Negro children in primary and secondary schools was illegal and had to be abolished. Even if there were no Voice of America, the news of this decision would resound to the farthest corners of the world.

The immediate reaction of newspapers, commentators, and other mass media was as automatic as a conditioned reflex. It was expressed in the ubiquitous headline: "Will South End Negro Schools?" But was this the only question raised by the clear-cut judgment of the Supreme Court? Was it even the most important one?

There were many forces on the scene and behind the scene that caused this historic decision. Here was a group of lawyers with superior skill, superior strategy, and devotion—and of course, a better case. They were organized and guided by Thurgood Marshall, the chief counsel of the National Association for the Advancement of Colored People, which handled the whole case. There were broad social contributing factors. Great economic changes have been going on; economists are not agreed on whether we are in a war economy heading for peace or a peace economy heading for war. Education of many for skilled work has become a necessity. In the last fifteen years or so, a new Negro middle class has developed. The South has made tremendous industrial strides forward; the time is past when it depended on the one-crop system of raising cotton. These and other economic circumstances of basic importance for the Supreme Court's decision will be fully disentangled only by future historians of our time.

Another causative element was the foreign reaction to racial discrimination in the United States. Extolling American democracy over the world was jammed less by physical sound waves than by the echoes of voices of people here suffering from racial discrimination. It was not without influence that the Chief Justice of the high court that arrived at this unanimous decision had never been a judge before in any court. This was a political decision as much as a legal one. Of course, some people see the Supreme Court's action in terms of a self-propelled mystical progress of culture. Perhaps they rely on [Gunnar] Myrdal's grandiose but abstract statement that "America is continually struggling for its soul." (Isn't that what Dr. Goebbels said about Nazi Germany?) Actually, history progresses along much more concrete lines. Long before this federal segregation case, there were many local skirmishes, social, legal, and administrative.

*

What will be the general effects of the Supreme Court decision? They are probably more varied than appears on the surface or in the headlines. The most immediate effect, unplanned and unforeseen, had little to do with the content of the judgment, coming rather from the painstaking and democratic legal way it was arrived at. At the Army-McCarthy hearings, legal and parliamentary procedures were being vitiated, distorted, and abused. Big issues were covered up by small talk, and little issues were inflated by big talk. Seasoned lawyers looking at the television screen squirmed at the disregard for orderly rules. With one stroke, the Supreme Court reestablished in the consciousness of the people the fact that there is a majesty of democratic law and an inviolability of due process.

The court also struck a blow at the idea, often expressed in different ways, that social change cannot be brought about by law. That is supposed to be a liberal view, but actually it is anarchy speaking. Of course, the world cannot be improved by law alone, but just as surely it cannot be improved without law. Both Thurgood Marshall and the N.A.A.C.P. know well how much progress in equalizing educational facilities has been made under legal duress. There is also the idea that you must view what is grandiosely called the "total picture" and that you cannot single out one factor, cannot attack one evil at a time. But the Supreme Court has just done this, and very successfully, though it could easily have sidestepped the issue, as most of us do.

Law is the best instrument for adult education. The old habit that you have to educate the people first and do the right thing afterward has now been exploded by the Supreme Court. The letter of the law can be interpreted, the spirit of the law can be violated, but the administration of the law is your affair through your voting for elected officials and through your spreading enlightenment, whether you live in the North or in the South.

Most important of all, it seems to me, is the lesson that goes beyond the issue of school segregation. The high court has given us a signal that there is a lot for all of us to do to counteract the race prejudice we see around us. There are many other areas where the classification rejected by the Supreme Court for schools still holds and prejudice reigns.

In some communities devoted to white people's recreation, Negroes, whoever they are, are not allowed on the street after 7 p.m. More race hatred has been instilled in American children through comic books in the past ten years than in the preceding hundred years. As Constance Curtis writes in her Harlem Diary: "From the time they can hold a book and look at a picture— long before they can read—the children are learning the most vicious stereotypes of the white superman and the dark degenerate." If race prejudice is outlawed in children's school hours, should not its instigation be outlawed in their time of leisure?

Much has to be done by all of us, in many areas of both private and public life. The Supreme Court has rendered its decision. The nine men have spoken. They have spoken to you.

The Supreme Court: Current
Criticism in Perspective

Maxwell Brandwen
May 24, 1958

The United States Supreme Court owes its existence to the
Constitution, but its appellate function—which represents, in
practice, most of its work—as well as its composition, are dependent on the will of Congress. Yet Congress is the very body whose
acts are reviewed by the Court. A coordinate branch of government, the Court is, in many respects, the weakest branch; it has
no power of purse and, even though it says what the law is, it
depends on other agencies of government for the enforcement of
its judgments. Yet, in some respects, it is the strongest because it is
charged with the responsibility of construing the Constitution—
the supreme law of the land. It is the ultimate lawgiver.

It is, therefore, unavoidable that the Court, girded with such
power, should be exposed to frequent attacks. Indeed, hardly
a decade has passed without violent agitation over its decisions since it was established in 1791. The rash of criticism
rose or fell synchronously with the degree of public interest in the decisions. At times, the attacks on the Court were
so serious that some jurisdictional powers were taken away
from it for a brief period. Even its size was manipulated by

Congress to meet particular political exigencies. At times, the attacks became so virulent and widespread that it seemed the institution would never regain its prestige and public confidence. But despite perennial controversy and disagreement, the Court's independence, jurisdiction, and authority have been fully maintained. It is a great tribute to the wisdom and restraint of Congress that this is so. Perhaps Congress' general laissez-faire policy may be due to the realization that the Court sooner or later somehow catches up with the political thinking of the large majority of the people. Indeed, at times, the Court may actually spur the thinking of the popular majority. In the long run, the views of the Court and of informed public opinion tend to harmonize.

Recently, there has been a marked revival of attacks on the Court because of its decisions during the past term. One Senator called for the impeachment of the Justices. Another termed the Court "a great menace to the country." A third called it "a politically motivated Court" and one which sought "to impress purely personal views on our social structure." Another suggested that the Justices submit to the necessity of reaffirmation from time to time. Still others demanded the reconstruction of the Court and restriction of its jurisdiction. Within the last month, a Senate committee, by a divided vote, approved a bill that would restrict the power of the Court in several directions.

Criticism has not been confined to Congress. It has been suggested that the power to appoint Justices be taken away from the President. A newspaper columnist proposed an investigation of the judges' law clerks, alleging that they play a significant role in the authorship of the Court's opinions. A cartoonist depicted one man saying to another: "What this country needs is a Super Supreme Court."

Surprisingly enough, sharp criticism came from dissenting members of the Court itself. One charged the Court with a "mischievous curbing of the informing function of the Congress." He also said that the Court's decision in the particular case involved would virtually cause government law-enforcement agencies to "close up shop" and would afford criminals "a Roman holiday." Another Justice charged the Court with "unacceptable intrusion" into matters which properly are within the purview of the states themselves. And a federal judge in South Carolina said that the Court "has been construing the Constitution so as to make it a protective shield for the criminally disposed and disloyal elements in our population."

*

There are those who say that the Court has gone too far in coddling the individual; the rights of the individual, they argue, must be subordinated to the greater welfare of the nation. There are others who say that the Court's restoration of the basic principles of individual dignity and liberty was long overdue. To them, these recent decisions are redolent of the glorious past— and symbolize a rebirth of faith.

There is considerable ground to believe that these decisions will remain solidly embedded in our jurisprudence. Of course, the landscaping of the decisions will undoubtedly be improved: a bit of pruning and paring here and there, a rough spot smoothed out, a gap filled in, a border more sharply trimmed. That is the customary fate of many judicial decisions.

The conclusion that these decisions will stand the test of time seems warranted by the vivid recognition of the rights of the individual, which spreads through their warp and woof. Sensitive regard for high ethical values permeates every cranny of the opinions. The decisions are in harmony with the traditional spirit of our country and show a sensitive regard for high ethical values. James Madison said: "Independent tribunals of justice ... will be naturally led to resist every encroachment upon rights expressly stipulated for in the Constitution." The Constitutional liberty and dignity of the individual are probably the most cherished tenets of our people. Our Courts are entrusted with their maintenance: Chief Justice Marshall pointed out that the law manifests "a tenderness for the rights of the individual." That this may not wither into an empty phrase is the never-ending task of the judiciary.

In retrospect, one may confidently say that the Court's finest hours were those in which it upheld and even extended the traditional rights of the individual. The preservation of our democratic system of government demands that the Court act as the knight-errant of individual Constitutional rights. People may differ as to whether there is as much freedom in our country as there was seventy-five years ago, but few will deny that the forces opposed to freedom are better organized today than they have been for some time.

Another point in favor of their survival is that they do not reflect sectional or political attitudes of particular Justices.

Three of the present Court were appointed by President Roosevelt, two by President Truman, and four by President Eisenhower. These men come from different parts of the land and from different backgrounds—political, academic, and judicial. That fact should help dispel the notion, wherever entertained, that their political attitudes had any bearing on their decisions. And there are men on the present Court of exceptional intellectual capacity.

*

Why, then, has there been such commotion about these decisions? It is because they deal with the age-old struggle between the individual and constituted authority. Striking a proper balance in that conflict is a most difficult task. It necessitates, as Justice Frankfurter says, "the exercise of impersonal judgment" buttressed, as far as is humanly possible, by historically-tried values. One may read and reread the Constitution from beginning to end, pore over the thousands and thousands of pages of judicial decisions, ponder the analyses of the countless scholars who have written on these matters, without finding a ready-made formula or a precise guide that would enable the Court to decide between the rights of the state and the rights of the individual. Some matters are beyond the compass of explicit definition.

Since the Constitution does not interpret itself, judgment "in the end," as Justice Frankfurter says, "cannot be escaped." Once the issues are joined, a judge may not take refuge in an ivory tower of suspended judgment. The Supreme Court must judge and resolve, even when a judgment would seem to tax the wisdom of a Solomon. That is the Court's peculiar burden, and the burden is made heavier because the Justices must view each decision not as an isolated phenomenon but as part of a whole legal fabric.

It is inherent in democracy and Constitutional government that decisions of the Court, which involve the balancing of powerful conflicting interests, will prove disappointing to some. Decisions of high Constitutional issues cannot be expected to command universal approval—even assuming that to be a desirable consummation. Certainly, all courts do and should respect the powers of Congress, but if their decisions are to be determined by the degree of satisfaction or disappointment felt by certain segments of Congress, then we will have truly abrogated our system of government. Neither pique nor notions of self-importance of public officials should be permitted to weaken the effectiveness of the Court itself as an institution of democracy.

*

It does not follow that decisions of the Court must be treated as sacred. There must be unremitting and unrelenting informed criticism of judicial decisions. The reasoning of courts may be shown to be faulty. Their misreading or misinterpretation of precedents should be clearly pointed out. Their disregard of pertinent considerations must be disclosed. All this is essential for the health and soundness of the Supreme Court as an important facet of our Constitutional government. But to suggest impeachment of Justices because one doesn't like a particular decision or to suggest that the Court is sabotaging the security of the country because a particular decision doesn't accord with the notions of a particular individual, however exalted he may be, is tantamount to advocating the end of government of laws. That is a frightening prospect and pregnant with the greatest danger to our country. There is a world of difference between contesting the soundness of a decision—that should be encouraged—and subjecting decisions to political control. One might take a leaf out of Abraham Lincoln's book. He condemned the decision of the Court in the *Dred Scott* case, but he did not allow himself the luxury of attacking the Court's integrity.

The Court, at times, undoubtedly has erred. Congress, at times, has erred too. The intelligent judgment of a future day may correct an erroneous decision of today, but political control of judicial decisions might open the floodgates to all manner of evils that could be corrected only by the greatest sacrifices of human dignity and even of human life. History has shown that the Court is concerned with, and is capable of, correcting its own errors and that it has served its historic purpose in protecting individual liberties from overzealous legislators and misguided Executive action.

The Justices of the Court, insulated as they must be from direct participation in public controversy, have remained silent in the face of attacks. But occasionally a Justice may allow himself the privilege of comment. Mr. Justice Holmes said in a lecture delivered in 1913: "It is very painful ... when one spends all the energies of one's soul in trying to do good work, with no thought but that of solving a problem according to the rules by which one is bound, to know that many see sinister motives...."

He continued with the following strong indictment: "The attacks upon the Court are merely an expression of the unrest that seems to wonder vaguely whether law and order pay. When the ignorant are taught to doubt they do not know what they may safely believe."

The Forgotten Amendment

James D. Carroll
September 6, 1965

In *Griswold v. Connecticut*, the birth-control case handed down on June 7, the Supreme Court confounded most of the informed members of its public by giving everyone something and no one everything. June 7 was one of those days when it was impossible to tell the good guys on the Court from the bad. While Justices Harlan and Black in the background were decorously exchanging the mantles of judicial restraint and judicial activism, in the foreground Justices Douglas and Goldberg were excitedly announcing the discovery of a general constitutional right to marital privacy and the rediscovery of the Ninth Amendment to the Constitution.

The Court's decision was clear and simple: seven members agreed that the Connecticut statute prohibiting the dissemination and use of birth-control information and devices is unconstitutional. The grounds on which the decision was reached were not so simple: the statute violates a right to marital privacy that is fundamental to our civilization and our way of life. To explain their reasoning, the seven members of the Court who agreed with the decision produced four opinions. The dissenting Justices Black and Stewart produced two. June 7 was a good day for those who like to read Supreme Court opinions.

It is evident that the appellants, Estelle T. Griswold and Dr. Charles Lee Buxton, had gotten what they wanted. The Planned Parenthood League's birth-control clinic in New Haven can now legally disseminate birth-control information and devices. The citizens of Connecticut can now practice birth control in peace. But the appellants paid for this victory, if not out of their own intellectual pockets, then out of the intellectual pockets of those who believe that some form of compulsory birth control will be necessary in the future. The price they paid was the Court's recognition of marital privacy as a right that transcends the social interests of the state. Three of the Court's liberals, Chief Justice Warren, Justice Goldberg, and Justice Brennan, went far out of their way to state flatly that a law requiring compulsory birth control would be just as unconstitutional as the Connecticut law outlawing voluntary birth control, since both laws would violate the right of marital privacy.

This observation was a dictum, of course, but it was no idle or academic dictum, nor was it a sop tossed to the beggars who wanted the Connecticut law upheld. These Justices expressed an acute awareness that many people in the United States and elsewhere are convinced that some form of compulsory birth control is inevitable. For example, Kenneth Boulding, who is widely and rightly respected as a thinker, recently outlined the world's population problem and explained his response to it: "I think in all seriousness," Boulding wrote in *The Meaning of the Twentieth Century*, "that a system of marketable licenses to have children is the only one which will combine the minimum of social control necessary to solve this problem with a maximum of individual liberty and ethical choice." Boulding's plan may seem absurd at the moment, but who fifty years ago could foresee that in the 1960s the Catholic Church would re-examine its stand on artificial birth control?

*

The grounds of the Court's decision should satisfy many citizens who wanted the Court to leave the Connecticut statute alone. Even those who think the Court should quit playing the role of interpreter of the American conscience should be pleased with the majority's affirmation of a right to marital privacy and with the clear suggestion that the majority will recognize other forms of a general right to privacy in the future.

Prior to the birth-control decision, a right to privacy had to be tagged on to one of the specific rights affirmed in the First, Third, Fourth, Fifth, or Sixth Amendments. If the action of a state were involved, the right had to be arrived at through interpretation of the due process clause of the Fourteenth Amendment. A central issue in the case was this: Is there a constitutional right to privacy that applies to both state and federal action involving relationships not enumerated in the Constitution?.

The majority of the Court held yes. The majority flatly stated that a constitutionally protected "zone of privacy" against state and federal action exists, a zone not limited to the exact relationships specified in specific constitutional provisions. In cases of state action, this zone of privacy is guaranteed both by the due process clause of the Fourteenth Amendment and by the Ninth Amendment. In cases of federal action, it is guaranteed by the entire Bill of Rights.

The boundaries of the zone of privacy will have to be defined in future cases. Those who regard the invasion of the individual's privacy through the collectivization of man as one of the great threats of our time may come to regard the Griswold case as the Magna Charta of the 20th century. In more modest terms, they may derive immediate solace from Justice Douglas' concluding words of the Court's opinion:

> We deal with a right of privacy older than the Bill of Rights— older than our political parties, older than our school system. Marriage is a coming together for better or for worse, hopefully enduring, and intimate to the degree of being sacred. The association promotes a way of life, not causes, a harmony in living, not political faiths; a bilateral loyalty, not commercial or social projects.

To the student of constitutional history, perhaps the most interesting aspect of the birth-control case is the Court's recognition of the Ninth Amendment as a mechanism for the expression of "the collective conscience of our people" against both federal and state action. The Ninth Amendment reads: "The enumeration in the Constitution, of certain rights, shall not be construed to deny or disparage others retained by the people." The recognition at this time of the Ninth Amendment as a substantive limitation on state and federal action is truly an astounding development. As Bennett B. Patterson pointed out ten years ago in *The Forgotten Ninth Amendment*, the Supreme Court throughout its entire history has almost completely ignored the Ninth Amendment.

*

As far as I can determine, from a recent check of Supreme Court cases, the Court never in its entire history has decided a single case on the basis of the Ninth Amendment. Throughout most of its history, the Court has apparently accepted the traditional understanding of the amendment expressed by Justice Stewart in his dissenting opinion in the birth-control case. Justice Stewart argued that the Ninth Amendment was adopted merely to make clear that the adoption of the Bill of Rights did not alter the plan that the federal government is a government of express and limited powers. "Until today, no member of this Court has ever suggested that the Ninth Amendment meant anything else..."

Justice Goldberg expressed the new meaning of the Ninth Amendment in his concurring opinion. He argued that the language and history of the Ninth Amendment reveal that the framers of the Constitution believed that other fundamental rights which are protected against government infringement exist alongside the rights specifically mentioned in the first eight amendments to the Constitution. The Ninth Amendment recognizes that these fundamental personal rights, such as the right to marital privacy, are protected from abridgment by government though not specifically mentioned in the Constitution. The courts must look to the "collective conscience of our people" to determine whether a principle is so rooted there as to be ranked as fundamental.

The recognition by the Court of the Ninth Amendment is of fundamental importance as an affirmation of the Court's intention to protect the sovereignty and dignity of the individual. In a way, this recognition constitutes the declaration of a new

Bill of Rights for the 20th century, for as Patterson said in his prophetic book:

> There is no clause in the Constitution, except the Ninth Amendment, which makes a declaration of the sovereignty and dignity of the individual. Since individual freedom is the basis of democracy, and is the virtue which marks the excellence of our form of government over all other forms of government ... the Ninth Amendment immediately takes its place as the most important declaration in our Constitution, because such a declaration is nowhere else therein to be found.

Who won the birth-control case? All of the parties to the case, both immediate and remote, lost something, but I personally think that in the Court's recognition of a constitutional right of privacy and in the Court's recognition of the Ninth Amendment, everyone gained a lot.

Jane Roe and Mary Doe

Editorial
February 5, 1973

It is not easy to get an appealed case as far as the Supreme Court of the United States; the Court does not concern itself with trivial matters. It is even rarer—probably unprecedented—for litigants to carry their appeals to the Court anonymously. Yet, two women, designated Jane Roe and Mary Doe, residents of Texas and Georgia, respectively, did just that—and won their cases. The reason for their anonymity was their desire for abortions, which were disallowed by the laws of their states. Mary, 22 years old and eleven weeks pregnant with her fourth child when she brought the action, was married. Jane's age was not given in the news reports, but she was unmarried. Now that they have prevailed on an issue of enormous religious, ethical, and social importance, they may choose to reveal their identities. However, their right to privacy in this respect, as well as their right not to bear children, has been upheld by the Court. They, and the seven Justices who voted in their favor, have performed a service of incalculable importance for American womanhood.

As a fringe benefit, they have taught the country a lesson in the practical workings of democracy, thus strengthening our system of government. As recently as ten years ago, it was inconceivable that such a decision could have been handed down. What are the prerequisites for such a reversal of attitude at the highest judicial level? For one thing, there must be a special constituency, imbued with zeal, equipped with reason, and pushing hard for a change in the law. Without an activist vanguard, ancient concepts will not be questioned, much less critically examined. In the matter of abortion, Planned Parenthood, Women's Lib, liberal gynecologists, and other groups provided the necessary motive power.

Then, the special constituency must have able and dedicated counsel who will painstakingly marshal not merely the law but the facts of the situation to show the weaknesses in the accepted way of doing things. This branch of law is far more exacting—and less financially rewarding—than, for instance, bankruptcy law.

Perseverance is essential. Counsel must be prepared to lose the first, second, and third rounds and continue without flagging. They must tire the appellate judges until they begin reflecting and develop a sense of guilt about the mistakes they and their predecessors have made and keep repeating. It requires patience, tenacity, dogged persistence, as well as intellect and skill in the law. When these are brought to bear, circumstances may favor those previously unfavored.

Before the courts can change, societal mores must change. A new consciousness must emerge. It may take decades, even generations, or it may come with amazing speed when time, acting through people, has done its work. Some aspects of this process are mysterious; others can be discerned with less difficulty, such as the exchange of experience from one generation to the next.

Judges have sons and daughters, nephews and nieces, and are often informed of developments of which they do not formally take "judicial knowledge."

In the abortion controversy, it became clear, also, that gross discrimination was involved: the rich had no problem, the poor did, and more particularly the black poor on welfare. Even more than health care generally, the right to abortion depended on the economic status of those who desired it. Often, also, a progressive cause benefits for dubious reasons as well as ethically acceptable ones—might not the increasing tax burden of the "bums on welfare" be kept in check if their reproduction could be checked? This may have been a factor in the passage by the New York State legislature of a liberal abortion law, which has been generally successful. The legislature was moved by many of the same forces that moved the Supreme Court. Because the Catholic Church was so vehemently opposed to abortion, it took a certain amount of courage for the Assemblymen and Senators to pass a liberal law and for Governor Rockefeller to resist attempts to repeal it.

The medical inputs are those of any technology—practice develops a body of specialists and improved techniques. New York City Health Department statistics show that complications of any kind—a headache rated as a complication—dropped from 4.6 per thousand the first year to 3.0 the second. On average, abortion is now safer than childbirth. Both the voluntary and proprietary abortion clinics in New York are on par with the best hospital practice, and the possibility of a reversion to back-alley abortion is so revolting as to border on the inconceivable.

The religious aspect remains unchanged by the Supreme Court decision. Those who wish to have children, a few or many, can still have them. They are free to try to convince their fellow citizens that the "right to life" is indivisible and paramount. But those who wish the Catholic Church well can only be dismayed by the insistence of the bishops, an exclusively male, celibate sodality, on a doctrine which almost half of Catholic women repudiate. A prime reason for the alienation of many formerly practicing Catholics is the opposition of the hierarchy to both contraception and abortion.

The Supreme Court decision does not go all the way. There will be renewed efforts to circumvent it. But it is a rebuke to President Nixon's letter of May 1972, flatly opposing "liberalized abortion policies," and a salutary reassertion of the independence of the Supreme Court, in that three of the four Justices appointed by Mr. Nixon voted with the majority.

PART THREE

Judicial Neanderthals

Nixon's Last Laugh: The Constitution in Retreat

Arthur S. Miller
April 10, 1976

Richard Nixon may be exiled to California, but his handiwork remains. One of the latest examples is the Supreme Court's decision on March 3 that a shopping center could not be used by a union as a site for its picket line. The decision, true enough, was written by Potter Stewart, an Eisenhower appointee, but he was joined by Nixonites Warren Burger, Lewis Powell, Harry Blackmun, and William Rehnquist. Only Thurgood Marshall and William Brennan dissented. The Nixon Court reigns supreme.

The decision, *Hudgens v. National Labor Relations Board*, is a major setback for attempts mounted in recent decades to apply constitutional guarantees—in this instance, freedom of speech—to private organizations that exercise significant social power or that present themselves as serving the public. The movement began for business corporations with the Court's 1946 holding that Chickasaw, Ala., a wholly owned company town, was subject to the First Amendment's guarantee of freedom of religion. A real breakthrough came in 1968, when the Court under Chief Justice Earl Warren held that union picketing on a private shopping center was protected by the First Amendment's freedom of speech.

Some commentators, myself among them, saw these cases as signaling the recognition of the concept of "private governments" under the Constitution—that, in other words, there are times when private groups wield so much power or are so closely tied to government that they should be considered part of government for the purposes of the Constitution. The retreat from that position began as soon as Nixon packed the Court. In 1972, it held that a group of Vietnam War protesters could not picket on a shopping center's property. The retreat has now become a rout, insofar as private corporations are concerned.

*

The constitutional concept is "state action," which means, in essence, that the Constitution runs against (public) government only. And so Justice Stewart said. He distinguished the company-town case and casually ignored some other law. It is settled beyond doubt, for example, that a political party is subject to constitutional restraints. A series of cases culminating in *Terry v. Adams* (1953) held that both sophisticated and simple-minded schemes to avoid the reach of the right to vote protected by the Constitution were invalid. And in the "sit-in" civil rights cases of the 1960s, the Court stretched the law to make restaurants and other places of public accommodation amenable to the Constitution.

It was, accordingly, disingenuous at best of Justice Stewart to say that "Our institutional duty is to follow until changed the law as it now is, not as some members of the Court might wish it to be." For he did state the law as he "might wish it to be"—the 1968 shopping-center case has now been expressly overruled. The 1972 case, *Lloyd Corp. v. Tanner*, did not apply to unions, which have long been held to have First Amendment protection for picketing. Stewart and his colleagues did not follow the law "as it now is"—as Justice Byron White pointed out in his concurring opinion.

Thus, Nixon succeeded in one aim: he packed the Court with ideologues, who are now in control. Stewart tends to be a waffler, to bend and sway with the wind; so he often joins the Nixonites. So does White, a Kennedy appointee. Only Thurgood Marshall and William Brennan hew to the line of the Warren Court.

Private corporations—the largest among them, at least—should long since have been restrained by the Constitution. General Motors and AT&T, to name only two of the biggest, have far more power—economic power, which in turn means political power—than, say, the allegedly sovereign states of Rhode Island and Delaware, which are subject to the Constitution. Were the Constitution to be rewritten today, there can be little doubt that the giant business firms, as well as such other influential groups as labor unions, would be made amenable to constitutional limitations.

The time has come, in other words, for a mutational leap to be made in our constitutional jurisprudence. When the Constitution was written in 1787, corporations were few and quite small; labor unions were unknown. Today Americans are governed in fact, if not in theory, as much by the private governments of the nation as by the public governments. This happens in two ways: first, the private economic entities make decisions of national importance, such as the direction and allocation of investment and resources. Second, private economic groups wield substantial influence over the way in which decisions are made within public government. Prof. Grant McConnell said it well in 1966: "A substantial part of government in the United States has come under the influence or control of narrowly based and largely autonomous elites."

The Supreme Court is refusing to recognize the enormous changes in the social order that have occurred in the past century. Justice Stewart's notion of property in the *Hudgens* case harks back to the bad old days when the Court, with invincible myopia, exalted property rights over human rights. That situation did not last then, and it should not last now, simply because it is absurd. Even Justices should know that. The "nine old men" of the 1930s have now been replaced by some judicial Neanderthals.

Burger's Court Feathers Its Nest

Robert G. Sherrill
June 24, 1978

Chief Justice Warren Burger's seemingly insatiable desire for publicity and his accompanying yen to manipulate the press and public opinion has on several recent occasions raised for the Supreme Court the unpleasant possibility that some of its future rulings could be seriously questioned as to objectivity. Under Burger's reign, the Court has done everything but hire a public relations firm to inflate its image. The ground floor of the Supreme Court building has been turned into a museum of flattering exhibits that—though tasteful on the whole—John Marshall would no doubt look upon as pandering to tourists. In 1971, Burger appointed William F. Swindler, a William and Mary law professor, as head of a group to create a "historical society" like those that puff up the White House and the Capitol. In 1974, accordingly, the Supreme Court Historical Society was incorporated, with Burger its honorary chairman, and the flood of puffery began. The SCHS will happily sell you a 3-inch, $8 bronze medallion of Burger. An SCHS fund-raising newsletter last year praised a *Smithsonian Magazine* story on the Court as "perhaps the most informative explanation of Supreme Court operations...in many years. Major portions of the article feature the responsibilities of Chief Justice Burger." Burger, by the way, is chancellor of the Smithsonian Institution's trustees. The Supreme Court Historical Society is selling reprints of the article, along with other gimcracks, to the Court's visitors.

All of this could be dismissed as just more of the standard Washington flackery, but there is a dark side to it. The SCHS actively solicits contributions from lawyers and businessmen. Presumably, Burger and other Justices watch the list of contributors to see who is generous ($5,000 will make you a "sponsor"; $50,000 makes you a "benefactor").

One of the life members of SCHS is Robert T. Stevens, who also, as it happens, is the society's chairman. He is especially generous, not only giving his time to promoting the Burger Court but also contributing $8,500 that the society might commission a painting of Burger for the National Portrait Gallery. Before he retired, Robert T. Stevens was head of J.P. Stevens Co., the textile firm that is, at the moment, the most notorious labor-baiting corporation in America. Unions have taken it to court dozens of times. When one of these cases reaches the U.S. Supreme Court, will Burger be embarrassed? Will he, more to the point, be influenced by his friendship with the chairman of the SCHS? William Delaney, the *Washington Star* reporter who first brought this unsettling relationship to the public's attention, had no trouble finding a public-interest lawyer who pondered, "It's surprising that Burger would want to be publicly associated with Stevens, as much as that firm is involved in labor litigation." Perhaps that is a contrived worry, and perhaps it isn't, but the relationship clearly doesn't enhance the Court's reputation for objectivity.

Should Supreme Court Nominees Have Opinions?

Sanford Levinson
October 17, 1981

Sandra Day O'Connor has been sworn in as a Justice of the Supreme Court, but her conduct during her confirmation hearings raises again an important issue that will be with us for a long time to come. That issue is the willingness of nominees to comment on cases previously decided by the Court.

This is far from a trivial matter. After all, five Supreme Court Justices are over 73, so it is quite possible that Ronald Reagan will appoint a majority of the Court before he leaves office. The 90-to-0 vote to confirm O'Connor, taken together with her reluctance to discuss her judicial philosophy as it applies to critical areas of social policy reflected in specific cases, continues dubious precedents. (In fairness to O'Connor, it should be noted that many of her predecessors, particularly in the post-World War II era, have claimed a similar exemption from substantive discussion of issues before the Supreme Court.) In her prepared statement to the Senate Judiciary Committee, O'Connor said:

> I do not believe that, as a nominee, I can tell you how I might
> vote on a particular issue which may come before the Court,
> or endorse or criticize specific Supreme Court decisions

presenting issues which may well come before the Court again. To do so would mean I have prejudged the matter or have morally committed myself to a certain position. Such a statement by me as to how I might resolve a particular issue or what I might do in a future Court action might make it necessary to disqualify myself on the matter.

The bulk of the senators' questions related to *Roe v. Wade*, the 1973 abortion case. Many supporters of abortion rights, I suspect, admired the way O'Connor deftly avoided revealing her views on that decision. Their admiration was shortsighted, however. It is altogether proper for senators who take their duties of advice and consent seriously to question prospective federal judges about significant problems of constitutional law and theory. Moreover, the reasons O'Connor offered for evading politically touchy questions do not stand up.

Obviously, no nominee should promise to vote one way or the other in a future case, but that is not the issue. What the senators (and the public) wish to know is whether the nominee has devoted serious thought to the Constitution. Such reflection will inevitably lead him or her to "endorse or criticize specific Supreme Court decisions."

Roe v. Wade was undoubtedly the most important constitutional decision of the past decade. It raised profound questions of constitutional interpretation, ranging from the ascription of meaning to the constitutional text (which does not mention "privacy," let alone "abortion") to the Supreme Court's role as enunciator of so-called "fundamental values." In addition, abortion is one of the most volatile issues in contemporary

American politics. Not to have views on *Roe v. Wade* is equivalent to not having views on the nature of the Constitution itself or on the nature of the Supreme Court's role in a constitutional system. It is as if a nominee to the Court in 1860 declined to comment on the *Dred Scott* decision, to which *Roe* is comparable in its implications.

If O'Connor had views on *Roe*, she had a duty to articulate them. As a lawyer, a legislator, and a judge, she had already sworn several times over to support, protect, and defend the Constitution of the United States. If she takes her oaths seriously, she must oppose unconstitutional acts wherever found, and by whomever committed, including her new colleagues on the Supreme Court. All she needed to say to the Senate was that her present view is that *Roe* is (or is not) a legitimate decision, leaving open the possibility that further reflection and argument will change her mind. She had no obligation to promise the senators that she would vote in a given way in a future case, but she did have the duty to tell them her current thoughts about the constitutionality of the *Roe* decision or of any other case decided by the Court.

Her argument about prejudgment is, to put it kindly, ludicrous. If taken seriously, it would disqualify all present Justices of the Court, save herself, since they have all taken vigorous public positions on the *Roe* case and those that followed it. (Can there be any doubt that Justices Harry Blackmun and William Rehnquist, to take the most obvious examples, have prejudged the abortion cases that will continue to come before the Court? More to the point, can we imagine any sitting judge not prejudging future cases in some significant sense?)

We also have to wonder how far O'Connor would extend her principle. What if a senator had asked her about *Marbury v. Madison*, the 1803 case in which Chief Justice John Marshall articulated the theory of judicial review of congressional legislation? That issue will also be before the Court during O'Connor's tenure in every case in which the constitutionality of a law passed by Congress is challenged. Marshall's reasoning in *Marbury* is hardly impeccable, and it would have been interesting indeed to hear O'Connor analyze the cogency of his argument. Would it have been proper for her to profess skepticism about *Marbury*?

Many Americans were outraged when President Dwight Eisenhower refused to firmly endorse *Brown v. Board of Education*, and it is all too easy to imagine our collective reaction should a future Reagan nominee to the bench refuse to support *Brown* on the ground that school desegregation cases will continue to come before the Court and thus there should be no prejudgment of the constitutional legitimacy of segregation. Loftier criteria than whose ox is being gored should govern our reactions to the questions judicial nominees are asked and to their responses (or evasions).

One also wonders how the questioning will be conducted in future confirmation hearings if O'Connor's no-comment policy is allowed to stand. For example, Robert Bork is reported to be a likely nominee to the Court of Appeals for the District of Columbia, and his former colleague at Yale, Ralph Winter, is a leading candidate for a seat on the U.S. Court of Appeals for the Second Circuit. Both men have written on many issues of law and have bitterly criticized specific Supreme Court decisions as usurpations of the powers of the legislative branch. Like most legal academics, including many "liberals," Bork has criticized the *Roe* decision. During testimony before a Senate committee in opposition to a bill declaring fetuses to be persons and stripping federal courts of most of their jurisdiction to hear abortion-related cases, he made it clear that he found *Roe* indefensible. Bork has also published a controversial (and frightening) article on the limits of the First Amendment, which included assessments of cases already decided.

Of course, it might be said that senators are politicians, not constitutional scholars. No doubt Senator John East was more interested in O'Connor's views on abortion than on constitutional theory. If so, we must demand that senators take their constitutional duties more seriously and not give judicial nominees a blank check to believe whatever they like about the Constitution.

If the Constitution is to continue to serve as the foundation of our political system, then it must be taken seriously by all actors in that system, from citizens to Supreme Court Justices. To leave constitutional interpretation to the Supreme Court is not only to engage in the most vulgar "realism"—i.e., the Constitution is (only) what the Court says it is—it is ultimately to give up the belief in a meaningful Constitution altogether.

However distasteful Senator East's political views, he was performing a public service by interrogating O'Connor, and she did not live up to her responsibilities as a potential member of our highest court. It is vital that her stonewalling not become binding precedent in future confirmation hearings.

The Frantic Reflagging of Bork

Herman Schwartz
September 19, 1987

The campaign to put Judge Robert Bork on the Supreme Court is built on a Big Lie: that Bork is a moderate, flexible centrist like retired Justice Lewis Powell Jr., whom he was nominated to replace. The White House, Washington corporate lawyer Lloyd Cutler and Bork himself have all worked industriously to cover up what Bork really is—a rigid far-right activist who is not at all hesitant about using whatever power he has to further his ideology.

A few weeks after President Reagan nominated Bork, Cutler rushed to print with a piece on the *New York Times* Op-Ed page. Writing as "a liberal Democrat and as an advocate of civil rights before the Supreme Court," Cutler placed Bork in the tradition of Justices Oliver Wendell Holmes, Louis Brandeis, Felix Frankfurter, Potter Stewart and Powell, asserting he would be "closer to the middle than to the right' of the Supreme Court spectrum. No matter that Bork disagrees with all those Justices on the central issues before the Court, that Bork has scathingly criticized Holmes and Brandeis for granting too much latitude to free expression, has ridiculed Brandeis's antitrust theories, deplored Powell's affirmative-action ruling in the Regents of the *University of California v. Bakke* case (and, by implication, his other decisions in that area), disagrees with Frankfurter's church-and-state views and has branded as illegitimate the rulings upholding abortion laws that Stewart and Powell have several times reaffirmed. For Cutler, Bork is "not far from the Justice whose chair he has been nominated to fill."

Eleven days later, the White House issued a thick briefing book that painted Bork as a "powerful ally of First Amendment values" and other civil liberties and rights, whose views were in the "mainstream." Statistics were compiled to show that he had dissented in only 6 percent of the cases that came before him. No mention was made of the fact that there is dissent in the Courts of Appeals decisions less than 4 percent of the time.

Bork himself has given interviews to a series of newspapers in which, while disclaiming any intention to discuss "issues," he made sure to get across the point that he was a "moderate centrist." His statements in an interview with *USA Today* were typical:

USA TODAY: Haven't you said you don't think of yourself as a conservative?

BORK: Not as a matter of legal point of view. The position I have taken in public—that you can find in my writing—is that the judge's task is to take the intentions of the legislatures and apply to the circumstances. It's a view that has been taken by liberals and a view that's been taken by conservatives —and it's a view that's been denied by both.

USA TODAY: Some people say that your being on the Supreme Court could flip a lot of precedents. And you'd say, don't necessarily bet on it.

BORK: Right.

Bork's writings have revealed a rigid reactionary, and part of the strategy to make him look like a moderate entails distinguishing between what he has said as a law professor and what he would do as a Justice. Thus, he told *USA Today*, "I think it's possible as an academic to toss out ideas with some freedom. But when you're a judge, what you're doing is important to people. You don't feel the same kind of intellectual freedom that you might as an academic."

Bruce Fein of the Heritage Foundation, a former associate deputy U.S. Attorney in the Reagan Administration and a spokesman for the right, was more candid. In an interview broadcast by the Voice of America, Fein disagreed sharply with Cutler:

> The Bork nomination would mean, by and large, the entire docket of the Court would turn a conservative hue, rather than just half, as it's been over the last decade. By and large, Presidents get what they want. I think Judge Bork would vote the way President Reagan would anticipate.

And Cutler's own credibility in this matter is somewhat suspect. As evidence of Bork's liberalism, he cited and quoted from Bork's opinion in *Ollman v. Evans and Novak*, in which Bork came out for expanding press freedom from libel suits when criticizing political figures. Last year, however, Cutler also testified that Antonin Scalia was a centrist. As evidence of Scalia's liberalism, he cited the same *Ollman* decision. The catch is that Scalia and Bork were on opposite sides in the *Ollman* case and had sharply disagreed.

Presidents have often tried to shape the Court in their image and, as Fein says, "usually successfully." Franklin D. Roosevelt transformed the Court with his appointments and Richard Nixon achieved what he intended. But both those Presidents' goals were limited. Roosevelt only wanted to halt the Court's interference with governmental efforts to direct the economy. Nixon's main goal was to overturn the Warren Court's criminal justice rulings.

Reagan's agenda is much broader than either Roosevelt's or Nixon's. He is trying virtually to end the Supreme Court's role in advancing individual rights. The Administration has not only attacked the Court's rulings on affirmative action, separation of church and state, abortion, equal protection and criminal justice; it has also challenged the legitimacy of the Court's entering these areas at all. Attorney General Edwin Meese 3d's verbal assaults on the incorporation doctrine (which requires state and local officials to adhere to the Bill of Rights); his rejection of the Supreme Court's traditional role as the ultimate expositor of the Constitution; and his criticism of decisions that depart from what he considers to be the "original intent" of the Constitution's framers are expressions of that attitude.

Bork's record, on and off the bench, is tailor-made for the Reagan Administration's agenda. Like Meese, he has assailed not only the specific rulings but their legitimacy. And his record on the bench shows that despite constant reiteration of his fidelity to "judicial restraint," he is aggressively activist in furthering his views, regardless of judicial precedent and even the clear will of Congress.

Bork's hostility to the Court's decisions on abortion, affirmative action and school prayer is well known. Less known are Bork's views on access to the courts, antitrust and discrimination; the White House and Cutler did not mention the first two and omitted much about the third.

A legacy of the Warren Court is the availability of a Federal forum for people injured by government or private misconduct. Since his first days on the bench, Bork has gone out of his way to undo that legacy. A study released by the A.F.L.-C.I.O. found that in seventeen out of seventeen nonunanimous cases raising access issues he used a variety of procedural techniques to deny a litigant his day in court. Lack of standing to sue and governmental immunity have been his favorite grounds. Even when a majority of judges have voted to throw out a case on the substance of the claim, Bork has written a separate opinion challenging the court's authority to hear the case.

Thus, Bork has held that the homeless have no right to challenge a decision by the Administration not to establish a "model shelter' as promised; that Medicare patients may not challenge an effort of the Department of Health and Human Services to prevent the courts from reviewing denials of claims; that Haitian refugees may not challenge a government policy of stopping refugees on the high seas; and that Congressmen may not challenge the President's use of the pocket veto.

One of the cardinal principles of judicial restraint is that, whenever possible, the case should be decided on nonconstitutional grounds. Bork has nonetheless relied on the Constitution in almost all his standing-to-sue decisions, despite the availability of nonconstitutional alternatives, so that if his views prevail, even if Congress wanted to grant some people the right to sue, it could not.

Bork's views on laws barring racial and sexual discrimination also show his authoritarian side. In a 1971 law journal, he wrote that "most of substantive [i.e., non-procedural] equal protection ... improper. ... The Supreme Court has no principled way of saying which non-racial inequalities are impermissible." Precedents, some set forty years ago, were challenged as "improper," including decisions protecting illegitimate children and welfare recipients; rulings prohibiting judicial enforcement of racially restrictive housing covenants, sterilization of selected groups of felons, and poll taxes, as well as the case mandating the one person, one vote principle. Although he has since tried to back away from those views by calling them "academic," he has also said that they represented the culmination of seven years' hard thinking and debate with his mentor, the late Yale Law School Professor Alexander Bickel. And this year he reiterated that "I do think the equal protection clause probably should be kept to things like race and ethnicity."

Bork might not try to put those precise views into effect, but they are based on a profound predisposition toward judicial immobility where the protection of individual rights is concerned, and a methodology he has never repudiated— that the only valid sources of constitutional law are the text, history and structure of the Constitution. Those predispositions will inevitably emerge in his decision-making on new issues that come before him.

Moral Majority leader Jerry Falwell has declared that "We are standing at the edge of history. Our efforts have always stalled at the door of the U.S. Supreme Court and [the Bork nomination] may be our last chance to influence this most important body." He's right, and not because Bork is a centrist.

Women Scorned

Katha Pollitt
November 4, 1991

She's a spurned woman. No, she's a lesbian. She's the naive
dupe of left-wing "interest groups." No, she's a female Iago
bringing down a noble Black man out of sheer spite. She's
emotionally unstable. No, she's too calm and collected. She
wanted anonymity—obviously, she has something to hide. She
came forward—obviously, she wants money, fame, a book
contract. Male and female, Black and white, Americans could
believe anything of Anita Hill, it seems, except that she was
telling the truth about what Clarence Thomas did and said to
her when she worked for him at the Department of Education
and the EEOC [Equal Employment Opportunity Commission].
Forced to choose between a woman who had nothing to gain
and a man who had everything to lose, a woman with a reputation for probity and a man who is a demonstrable hypocrite,
a man who says he has never discussed *Roe v. Wade* with anyone on earth and who claims not to have written, intended,
or possibly even understood the ideas and opinions published
under his name, most people found him the more believable.
Is it any wonder women are reluctant to bring harassment
charges against men? In countries governed by Islamic fundamentalists, the testimony of a woman is officially given half

the legal weight as that of a man. We've come a long way, baby, haven't we?

Now the psychodrama is over. Her four impeccable, sober witnesses versus his panel of office harpies. John Doggett [a friend of Thomas who testified before the Senate], the walking personification of male vanity, insinuating that Anita Hill is still thinking about him ten years after he stood her up for dinner. [Wyoming Republican senator] Alan Simpson with his McCarthyite allusions to evidence he never reveals. [Utah Republican senator] Orrin Hatch with his quotes from *The Exorcist*. [Ohio Democratic senator] Howard Metzenbaum fumbling on about leaks, while his fellow Democrats, again and again, seemed to forget where they were and which side they were supposed to be on. Clarence Thomas is our new Supreme Court Justice, and we are left with the hard realities of power politics—the ball the Republicans never, for a moment, lost sight of, the ball the image-obsessed Democrats dropped when it was, for a moment, in their hands. The women who pooh-poohed Anita Hill will soon get their thank-you note: the reversal of *Roe v. Wade*. The African-American majority who supported Thomas on racial grounds will get their thank-you note as well: a Black hand, rather than a white one, penning the decisions abolishing the civil rights revolution.

Look on the bright side, women are being told. On PBS, Catharine MacKinnon took comfort from polls showing that 24 percent of Americans believed Anita Hill; ten years ago, it would have been zero. Finally, the sea change in gender relations has lapped at the halls of power, and the 98 percent male composition of the Senate has been shown, decisively, to have real consequences. It's a good thing, I suppose, that senators of all political stripes felt compelled to recognize and decry the everyday sexual humiliation of working women. But mostly it was just theater, hard-boiled men pretending to be shocked by words like "penis" and "pubic hair." These are the same men who have exempted themselves from civil rights and sexual harassment regulations and who can't get it together to pass civil rights legislation over President Bush's veto. They may condemn sexual harassment, but they don't care about it, and they don't understand it. As the time to vote on Thomas's confirmation drew near, senator after senator professed himself baffled that a woman would put up with demeaning remarks in order to keep her career on track, as if they themselves would never kowtow to, say, the gun lobby, or swallow their pride before a hated committee chairman.

The Op-Ed pages are full of sexual harassment now—outraged essays by women, balanced with jocular essays by men who wonder how they'll dare now to ask out a co-worker without Long Dong Silver [a British porn actor whose films Thomas had allegedly told his then-employee Anita Hill he enjoyed watching] as an icebreaker. But this is more theater, more psychodrama. The real story on sexual harassment is this: On the same day that *The New York Times* reported Thomas's confirmation, it also reported that California Governor Pete Wilson vetoed a bill that would have made it easier for victims of job discrimination—including sexual harassment—to sue for damages.

The political lesson of the Thomas confirmation goes way beyond the obvious fact that powerful men see the world differently from powerless women and should not be running the country like a frat house. Of course, we need more women in government. Of course, women ought to demand more of politicians who seek their vote. We do indeed need to rethink the lesser-of-two-evils philosophy that has brought to the Senate liberals like Daniel Patrick Moynihan, who benignly neglects all the reproductive-rights legislation currently languishing in Congress and who kept his office phones off the hook all weekend while he worked up his courage to vote against Thomas. And while we're at it, we need to rethink the never-mind-his-private-life philosophy too. The end result of that bit of fake pragmatism was Teddy Kennedy deliquescing into his chair as the hearings rolled on around him, reduced to virtual silence by his scandalous history, now capped by the supreme irony that his nephew's lawyers are currently using the same mudslinging tactics against the Palm Beach woman that Hatch and Simpson were using against Anita Hill. [Earlier that year, William Kennedy Smith had been accused of raping a woman on a beach in Florida. He was later acquitted.]

But we also need to be on our guard against the assumption that more women in Congress means more feminism. [Kansas Republican senator] Nancy Landon Kassebaum—half the women in the Senate—voted for Thomas. Yes, seven Congresswomen marched over to the Senate to convey their outrage at the Judiciary Committee's indifference to Anita Hill's charges at the time of the original hearings. But twenty-two stayed in their seats.

The real lesson, it seems to me, is that the Democratic Party is neither able nor willing to mount an effective opposition to the ongoing right-wing revolution. It's too compromised, too timid, too incompetent, too obsessed with courting the mythical center—too vested, in the end, in phony bipartisan statesmanship to do more than offer, in effect, a slow-motion version of the Reagan-Bush agenda. The men who rise to power through the Democratic Party will never be the means by which changing social relations between the sexes can enter the political process in a real way.

But it's too easy to rail at Congress. It may not be quite true that you get the government you deserve, but it's true enough. We need to elect more feminists and to refuse to vote for anyone, male or female, who does not embrace the expansion of our rights and only promises to delay their demise. We also need to create a militant movement outside the realm of representative politics. That is what AIDS activists have done. If ACT UP can force the FDA to change its drug protocols, women can force change through action. One-third of women sexually harassed at work? We can clog the courts with cases, we can confront harassers at the workplace as a group, we can boycott and take to the streets. We can picket hospitals that refuse to perform abortions—as 90 percent of them now do.

Of course, ACT UP activists are fighting for their lives. They don't have much time. Women and the men who care about them need to realize that we don't have much time either.

A Thousand Cuts

Editorial
July 20/27, 1992

This week's Supreme Court ruling in *Planned Parenthood v. Casey*, the Pennsylvania abortion case, managed to uphold *Roe v. Wade* on paper while eviscerating it in practice. True, the Court struck down the galling husband-notification requirement. But it upheld four other provisions—a twenty-four-hour waiting period, a mandatory antiabortion lecture from a doctor, parental consent for minors, and detailed record-keeping requirements. The Court thus gave its approval to state attempts to strew the path to abortion with obstacles in the hope that many women will not be able to surmount them.

Much has been made of the fact that three Reagan/Bush appointees—Sandra Day O'Connor, David Souter, and Anthony Kennedy—joined with Harry Blackmun and John Paul Stevens in affirming abortion as a constitutionally protected liberty, even as the trio stripped it of its status as a "fundamental" right. This is hardly the "moderate" and "centrist" position described in the press. *Roe* specifically barred restrictions on first and second trimester abortion that are unrelated to a woman's health; by permitting such restrictions, the Court in effect overturns *Roe*. It's as if the Court reaffirmed the First Amendment while upholding a state requirement that citizens wait twenty-four hours before making a speech.

That the decision is being touted as middle of the road shows how far to the right the road has swerved, but it could have been worse. (And it may yet be. Four justices—including Clarence Thomas—want to throw *Roe* out, and Justice Blackmun is 83.)

There's another reason, though, that many people may not recognize *Casey* as a serious threat to legal abortion. After twenty years of anti-choice propaganda, abortion is now firmly associated in the public mind with tragedy, regret, emotional turmoil, and stress. Even pro-choicers have adopted this language to counter the image of women who have abortions as feckless and frivolous. But if abortion is so grave and momentous an act, if the decision is so difficult, what's so bad about making women "take time to reflect" and hear "both sides"? It's easy to lose sight of the fact that what proponents of restrictions really want is to get rid of abortion entirely—if not by outlawing it outright, then by inflicting death by a thousand cuts. Since the Pennsylvania restrictions weigh most heavily on the young, the rural, and the poor, middle-class urban voters may not grasp how onerous they are. A twenty-four-hour wait is not a problem if the clinic is around the corner and open every day. But what if it means two 100-mile trips, hotel and child-care expenses, an elaborate cover story, and a weeklong delay?

The good news is that by refusing formally to overturn *Roe* in a presidential election year, the Court has revealed that it is in fact not deaf to politics. The challenge for pro-choicers is to persuade voters that the slow bleeding of *Roe* will be as fatal to abortion rights as decapitation with a single blow.

PART FOUR

Rightward Tilt

"None Dare Call It Treason"

Vincent Bugliosi
February 5, 2001

In the December 12 ruling by the US Supreme Court handing the election to George Bush, the Court committed the unpardonable sin of being a knowing surrogate for the Republican Party instead of being an impartial arbiter of the law. If you doubt this, try to imagine Al Gore's and George Bush's roles being reversed and ask yourself if you can conceive of Justice Antonin Scalia and his four conservative brethren issuing an emergency order on December 9 stopping the counting of ballots (at a time when Gore's lead had shrunk to 154 votes) on the grounds that if it continued, Gore could suffer "irreparable harm," and then subsequently, on December 12, bequeathing the election to Gore on equal protection grounds. If you can, then I suppose you can also imagine seeing a man jumping away from his own shadow, Frenchmen no longer drinking wine.

From the beginning, Bush desperately sought, as it were, to prevent the opening of the door, the looking into the box—unmistakable signs that he feared the truth. In a nation that prides itself on openness, instead of the Supreme Court doing everything within its power to find a legal way to open the door and box, they did the precise opposite in grasping, stretching and searching mightily for a way, any way at all, to aid their choice for President, Bush, in the suppression of the truth, finally settling, in their judicial coup d'état, on the untenable argument that there was a violation of the Fourteenth Amendment's equal protection clause—the Court asserting that because of the various standards of determining the voter's intent in the Florida counties, voters were treated unequally, since a vote disqualified in one county (the so-called undervotes, which the voting machines did not pick up) may have been counted in another county, and vice versa. Accordingly, the Court reversed the Florida Supreme Court's order that the undervotes be counted, effectively delivering the presidency to Bush.

Now, in the equal protection cases I've seen, the aggrieved party, the one who is being harmed and discriminated against, almost invariably brings the action. But no Florida voter I'm aware of brought any action under the equal protection clause claiming he was disfranchised because of the different standards being employed. What happened here is that Bush leaped in and tried to profit from a hypothetical wrong inflicted on someone else. Even assuming Bush had this right, the very core of his petition to the Court was that he himself would be harmed by these different standards. But would he have? If we're to be governed by common sense, the answer is no. The reason is that just as with flipping a coin you end up in rather short order with as many heads as tails, there would be a "wash" here for both sides, i.e., there would be just as many Bush as Gore votes that would be counted in one county yet disqualified in the next. (Even if we were to assume, for the sake of argument, that the wash wouldn't end up exactly, 100 percent even, we'd still be dealing with the rule of *de minimis non curat lex*—the law does not concern itself with trifling matters.) So what harm to Bush was the Court so passionately trying to prevent by its ruling other than the real one: that he would be harmed by the truth as elicited from a full counting of the undervotes?

And if the Court's five-member majority was concerned not about Bush but the voters themselves, as they fervently claimed to be, then under what conceivable theory would they, *in effect*, tell these voters, "We're so concerned that *some* of you undervoters may lose your vote under the different Florida county standards that we're going to solve the problem by making sure that *none* of you undervoters have your votes counted"? Isn't this exactly what the Court did?

The Court majority, *after knowingly transforming* the votes of 50 million Americans into nothing and throwing out all of the Florida undervotes (around 60,000), actually wrote that their ruling was intended to preserve "the fundamental right" to vote. This elevates audacity to symphonic and operatic levels. The Court went on to say, after stealing the election from the American people, "None are more conscious of the vital limits on its judicial authority than are the members of this Court, and none stand more in admiration of the Constitution's design to leave the selection of the President to the people." Can you imagine that? As they say, "It's enough to drive you to drink."

What makes the Court's decision even more offensive is that it warmly embraced, of all the bitter ironies, the equal protection clause, a constitutional provision tailor-made for blacks that these five conservative Justices have shown no hospitality to when invoked in lawsuits by black people, the very segment

89

of the population most likely to be hurt by a Bush administration. As University of Southern California law professor Erwin Chemerinsky noted: "The Rehnquist Court almost never uses equal protection jurisprudence except in striking down affirmative action programs [designed to help blacks and minorities]. I can't think of a single instance where Scalia or Thomas has found discrimination against a racial minority, or women, or the aged, or the disabled, to be unconstitutional."

*

Varying methods to cast and count votes have been going on in every state of the union for the past two centuries, and the Supreme Court has been as silent as a church mouse on the matter, never even hinting that there might be a right under the equal protection clause that was being violated. Georgetown University law professor David Cole said, "[The Court] created a new right out of whole cloth and made sure it ultimately protected only one person—George Bush." The simple fact is that the five conservative Justices did not have a judicial leg to stand on in their blatantly partisan decision. As Yale law professor Akhil Reed Amar noted, the five conservative Justices "failed to cite a single case that, on its facts, comes close to supporting its analysis and result."

If the Court majority had been truly concerned about the equal protection of all voters, the real equal protection violation, of course, took place when they cut off the counting of the undervotes. As indicated, that very act denied the 50 million Americans who voted for Gore the right to have their votes count at all.

Other than the unprecedented and outrageous nature of what the Court did, nothing surprises me more than how it is being viewed by the legal scholars and pundits who have criticized the opinion. As far as I can determine, most *have* correctly assailed the Court for issuing a ruling that was clearly political. As the December 25 *Time* capsulized it, "A sizable number of critics, from law professors to some of the Court's own members, have attacked the ruling as...politically motivated." A sampling from a few law professors: Vanderbilt professor Suzanna Sherry said, "There is really very little way to reconcile this opinion other than that they wanted Bush to win." Yale's Amar lamented that "for Supreme Court watchers this case will be like BC and AD. For many of my colleagues, this was like the day President Kennedy was assassinated. Many of us [had] thought that courts do not act in an openly political fashion." Harvard law professor Randall Kennedy called the decision "outrageous."

The only problem I have with these critics is that they have merely lost respect for and confidence in the Court. "I have less respect for the Court than before," Amar wrote. The *New York Times* said the ruling appeared "openly political" and that it "eroded public confidence in the Court." Indeed, the always accommodating and obsequious (in all matters pertaining to the High Court, in front of which he regularly appears) Harvard law professor Laurence Tribe, who was Gore's chief appellate lawyer, went even further in the weakness of his disenchantment with the Court. "Even if we disagree" with the Court's ruling, he said, Americans should "rally around the decision."

Sometimes the body politic is lulled into thinking along unreasoned lines. The "conventional wisdom" emerging immediately after the Court's ruling seemed to be that the Court, by its political ruling, had only lost a lot of credibility in the minds of many people. But these critics of the ruling, even those who flat-out say the Court "stole" the election, apparently have not stopped to realize the inappropriateness of their tepid position vis-à-vis what the Court did. You mean you can steal a presidential election and your only retribution is that some people don't have as much respect for you, as much confidence in you? That's all? If, indeed, the Court, as the critics say, made a politically motivated ruling (which it unquestionably did), this is tantamount to saying, and can *only* mean, that the Court did not base its ruling on the law. And if this is so (which again, it unquestionably is), this means that these five Justices *deliberately and knowingly* decided to nullify the votes of the 50 million Americans who voted for Al Gore and to steal the election for Bush. Of course, nothing could possibly be more serious in its enormous ramifications. The stark reality, and I say this with every fiber of my being, is that the institution Americans trust the most to protect its freedoms and principles committed one of the biggest and most serious crimes this nation has ever seen—pure and simple, the theft of the presidency. And by definition, the perpetrators of this crime *have* to be denominated criminals.

*

Since the notion of five Supreme Court Justices being criminals is so alien to our sensibilities and previously held beliefs, and since, for the most part, people see and hear, as Thoreau said, what they expect to see and hear, most readers will find my characterization of these Justices to be intellectually incongruous. But make no mistake about it, I think my background in the criminal law is sufficient to inform you that Scalia, Thomas et al. are criminals in the very *truest* sense of the word.

Essentially, there are two types of crimes: *malum prohibitum* (wrong because they are prohibited) crimes, more popularly called "civil offenses" or "quasi crimes," such as selling liquor after a specified time of day, hunting during the off-season, gambling, etc.; and *malum in se* (wrong in themselves) crimes. The latter, such as robbery, rape, murder and arson, are the only true crimes. *Without exception, they all involve morally reprehensible conduct.* Even if there were no law prohibiting such conduct, one would know (as opposed to a *malum prohibitum* crime) it is wrong, often evil. Although the victim of most true crimes is an individual (for example, a person robbed or raped), such crimes are considered to be "wrongs against society." This is why the plaintiff in all felony criminal prosecutions is either the state (*People of the State of California v. _____*) or the federal government (*United States of America v. _____*).

No technical true crime was committed here by the five conservative Justices only because no Congress ever dreamed of enacting a statute making it a crime to steal a presidential election. It is so far-out and unbelievable that there was no law, then, for these five Justices to have violated by their theft of the election. But if what these Justices did was not "morally reprehensible" and a "wrong against society," what would be? In terms, then, of natural law and justice–the protoplasm of all eventual laws on the books—these five Justices are criminals in every *true* sense of the word, and in a fair and just world belong behind prison bars as much as any American white-collar criminal who ever lived. Of course, the right-wing extremists who have saluted the Court for its theft of the election are the same type of people who feel it is perfectly all right to have a mandatory minimum sentence of ten years in a federal penitentiary for some poor black in the ghetto who is in possession of just fifty grams of crack cocaine, even if he was not selling it.

*

Though the five Justices clearly are criminals, no one is treating them this way. As I say, even those who were outraged by the Court's ruling have only lost respect for them. And for the most part the nation's press seems to have already forgotten and/or forgiven. Within days, the Court's ruling was no longer the subject of Op-Ed pieces. Indeed, just five days after its high crime, the caption of an article by Jean Guccione in the *Los Angeles Times* read, "The Supreme Court Should Weather This Storm." The following day an AP story noted that Justice Sandra Day O'Connor, on vacation in Arizona, had fired a hole-in-one on the golf course.

The lack of any valid legal basis for their decision and, most important, the fact that it is inconceivable they would have ruled the way they did for Gore, proves, *on its face*, that the five conservative Republican Justices were up to no good. Therefore, not one stitch of circumstantial evidence beyond this is really necessary to demonstrate their felonious conduct and state of mind. (The fact that O'Connor, per the *Wall Street Journal*, said before the election that she wanted to retire but did not want to do so if a Democrat would be selecting her successor, that Thomas's wife is working for the conservative Heritage Foundation to help handle the Bush transition and that Scalia's two sons work for law firms representing Bush is all unneeded trivia. We already know, without this, exactly what happened.)

The bottom line is that nothing is more important in a democracy than the right to vote. Without it there cannot be a democracy. And implicit in the right to vote, obviously, is that the vote be counted. Yet with the election hanging in the balance, the highest court in the land ordered that the valid votes of thousands of Americans *not* be counted. That decision gave the election to Bush. When Justice Thomas was asked by a skeptical high school student the day after the Court's ruling whether the Court's decision had anything to do with politics, he answered, "Zero." And when a reporter thereafter asked Rehnquist whether he agreed with Thomas, he said, "Absolutely, absolutely." Well, at least we know they can lie as well as they can steal.

*

If there are two sacred canons of the right-wing in America and ultraconservative Justices like Scalia, Thomas and Rehnquist, it's their ardent federalism, i.e., promotion of states' rights (Rehnquist, in fact, wrote in his concurring opinion about wanting, wherever possible, to "defer to the decisions of state courts on issues of state law"), and their antipathy for Warren Court activist judges. So if it weren't for their decision to find a way, any way imaginable, to appoint Bush President, their automatic predilection would have been to stay the hell out of

Florida's business. The fact that they completely departed from what they would almost reflexively do in ninety-nine out of a hundred other cases is again persuasive circumstantial evidence of their criminal state of mind.

Perhaps nothing Scalia et al. did revealed their consciousness of guilt more than the total lack of legal stature they reposed in their decision. Appellate court decisions, particularly those of the highest court in the land, *all* enunciate and stand for legal principles. Not just litigants but the courts themselves cite prior holdings as support for a legal proposition they are espousing. But the Court knew that its ruling (that differing standards for counting votes violate the equal protection clause) could not possibly be a constitutional principle cited in the future by themselves, other courts or litigants. Since different methods of counting votes exist throughout the fifty states (e.g., Texas counts dimpled chads, California does not), forty-four out of the fifty states do not have uniform voting methods, and voting equipment and mechanisms in all states necessarily vary in design, upkeep and performance, to apply the equal protection ruling of *Bush v. Gore* would necessarily invalidate virtually all elections throughout the country.

This, obviously, was an extremely serious problem for the felonious five to deal with. What to do? Not to worry. Are you ready for this one? By that I mean, are you sitting down, since if you're standing, this is the type of thing that could affect your physical equilibrium. Unbelievably, the Court wrote that its ruling was *"limited to the present circumstances,* for the problem of equal protection in election processes generally presents many complexities." (That's pure, unadulterated moonshine. The ruling sets forth a very simple, noncomplex proposition–that if there are varying standards to count votes, this violates the equal protection clause of the Fourteenth Amendment.) In other words, the Court, in effect, was saying its ruling "only applied to those future cases captioned *Bush v. Gore*. In all other equal protection voting cases, litigants should refer to prior decisions of this court." Of the thousands of potential equal protection voting cases, the Court was only interested in, and eager to grant relief to, one person and one person only, George W. Bush. Is there any limit to the effrontery and shamelessness of these five right-wing Justices? This point, all alone and by itself, clearly and unequivocally shows that the Court knew its decision was not based on the merits or the law, and was solely a decision to appoint George Bush President.

*

Conservatives, the very ones who wanted to impeach Earl Warren, have now predictably taken to arguing that one shouldn't attack the Supreme Court as I am because it can only harm the image of the Court, which we have to respect as the national repository for, and protector of, the rule of law, the latter being a sine qua non to a structured, nonanarchistic society. This is just so much drivel. Under what convoluted theory do we honor the rule of law by ignoring the violation of it (here, the sacred, inalienable right to vote of all Americans) by the Supreme Court? With this unquestioning subservience-to-authority theory, I suppose the laws of the Third Reich—such as requiring Jews to wear a yellow Star of David on their clothing—should have been respected and followed by the Jews. Blacks should have respected Jim Crow laws in the first half of the twentieth century. Naturally, these conservative exponents of not harming the Supreme Court, even though the Court stole a federal election disfranchising 50 million American citizens, are the same people who felt no similar hesitancy savaging the President of the United States not just day after day, but week after week, month after month, yes, even year after year for having a private and consensual sexual affair and then lying about it. And this was so even though the vitriolic and never-ending attacks crippled the executive branch of government for months on end, causing incalculable damage to the office of the presidency and to this nation, both internally and in the eyes of the world.

These five Justices, by their conduct, have forfeited the right to be respected, and only by treating them the way they deserve to be treated can we demonstrate our respect for the rule of law they defiled, and insure that their successors will not engage in similarly criminal conduct.

Why, one may ask, have I written this article? I'll tell you why. I'd like to think, like most people, that I have a sense of justice. In my mind's eye, these five Justices have gotten away with murder, and I want to do whatever I can to make sure that they pay dearly for their crime. Though they can't be prosecuted, I want them to know that there's at least one American out there who knows (not thinks, but knows) precisely who they are. I want these five Justices to know that because of this article, which I intend to send to each one of them by registered mail, there's the exponential possibility that when many Americans look at them in the future, they'll be saying, "Why are these people in robes seated above me? They all belong behind bars." I want these five Justices to know that this is America, not a banana republic, and in the United States of America, you simply cannot get away with things like this.

At a minimum, I believe that the Court's inexcusable ruling will severely stain its reputation for years to come, perhaps decades. This is very unfortunate. As Justice Stevens wrote in his dissent: "Although we may never know with complete certainty the identity of the winner of this year's presidential election, the identity of the loser is perfectly clear. It is the nation's confidence in [this Court] as an impartial guardian of the rule of law." Considering the criminal intention behind the decision, legal scholars and historians should place this ruling above the Dred Scott case and *Plessy v. Ferguson* in egregious sins of the Court. The right of every American citizen to have his or her vote counted, and for Americans (not five unelected Justices) to choose their President was callously and I say criminally jettisoned by the Court's majority to further its own political ideology. If there is such a thing as a judicial hell, these five Justices won't have to worry about heating bills in their future. If the softest pillow is a clear conscience, these five Justices are in for some hard nights. But if they aren't troubled by what they did, then we're dealing with judicial sociopaths, people even more frightening than they already appear to be.

Roberts' Chill Heart

Bruce Shapiro
August 15/22, 2005

Is Judge John Roberts worth a fight? That's the question Senate
Democrats and civil rights lobbyists were asking as the amia-
ble nominee made his let's-get-acquainted rounds on Capitol
Hill. To put it bluntly: With Judge Roberts's reputation as a
skilled and unimpeachable Supreme Court litigator, with his
long bipartisan list of Washington friends, with George W.
Bush sure to appoint another conservative if he's defeated,
why bother?

Call as witness Ansche Hedgepeth, a 12-year-old girl who in
2000 made the mistake of eating a french fry on the Washington
Metro while police were in the midst of a quality-of-life crack-
down. Officers arrested Ansche, handcuffed her, threw her
in the back of a squad car and kept her in lockup for three
hours. This big-government approach to childrearing offended
Ansche's mother as well as the conservative Rutherford Institute
of Virginia, which sued on her behalf. The case ended up before
Judge Roberts, who refused to expunge her record. Why?
Arresting Ansche, he wrote, advanced "the legitimate goal of
promoting parental awareness and involvement with children
who commit delinquent acts."

How will this judge, who endorses the manacling of a youngster over a snack, rule when confronted with the profound civil liberties challenges of the "war on terror"? We don't need to speculate. The day after his interview with Bush, Roberts and two other Reagan/Bush appointees on the DC Circuit reinstated military tribunals at Guantánamo—ruling that courts have no authority to review the White House's determination to deny those prisoners Geneva Convention protections.

Together these two very different cases give the lie to any suggestion that Judge Roberts lacks a track record. Enthusiastic expansion of the power of the executive branch, whether in the guise of policing or the presidency, is the most consistent thread of Roberts's career. In this sense he's no conservative; he's an apostle of big and often unreviewable government—the perfect nominee for a White House that excluded military lawyers, the State Department and even John Ashcroft's top aides from the inner circles of post-9/11 justice policy. The Guantánamo ruling was a stunning embrace of the Administration's expansive view of presidential power, placing the Guantánamo tribunals beyond reach of Congress or courts. It is a refutation, as well, of international law, stripping courts of the ability to enforce a treaty.

Another lie about Roberts's nomination is the notion that his most contentious statements should be written off as a lawyer's responsibility to his clients, not reflections of personal conviction. Exhibit A in this argument is Roberts's now-famous footnote in *Rust v. Sullivan*, the 1991 health clinic "gag rule" case in which he argued as deputy solicitor general that *Roe v. Wade* was "wrongly decided and should be overruled." Just doing my job, just reflecting Administration policy, Roberts said in his 2003 confirmation hearing as an appellate judge—a line repeated by Republicans and Democrats alike in recent days. In fact, the *Rust v. Sullivan* footnote went so far and so enthusiastically outside any argument relevant to the case that Roberts might fairly be accused of politicizing his briefs. But leave that aside. The real issue is that Roberts was hardly a passive receptacle, a mouthpiece without conviction. At the time of *Rust v. Sullivan* Roberts had been designated by Ken Starr as his "political" deputy—running interference on sensitive policy issues that otherwise would have been left to career officials. It was a job that didn't exist in either the Carter or Clinton administrations. The White House and Starr trusted Roberts not just to reflect legal policy but to make it.

Which gets us to another lie. At this writing the White House has agreed to release some historical documents from the Reagan years, but it claims that Roberts's memos as deputy solicitor general are a matter of attorney-client privilege. But attorney-client privilege ends where policy-making begins. The Judiciary Committee has every reason to wonder about the role of the political deputy. Senators have every reason to inquire about the language Roberts used when crafting that argument against Roe. The reasoning a Supreme Court nominee brought to fighting against strong Voting Rights Act enforcement, to ending school desegregation and to stripping Congress of oversight of federal environmental enforcement are all matters of public concern.

Roberts's professional biography suggests that every political choice he has made has been partisan and often rigidly ideological, from his clerkship with William Rehnquist through his role as a Republican adviser in *Bush v. Gore*. (Memo to Judiciary Committee: There's nothing out of bounds in asking Roberts's view of that case and whether he thinks the Supreme Court majority's ruling amounted to judicial activism.) Vigorous opposition to Roberts offers a powerful lesson on the intersection of politics and law in Bush's Washington. Bush may not have had a "litmus test" on *Roe v. Wade*, but he was precise about the political chemistry of his nominees. It's revealing that virtually all those floated as Supreme Court finalists were members of the Federalist Society. Roberts may not–or may–have been a member (at this writing the White House uses the deniable "no recollection" to explain why his name shows up in the group's confidential leadership directory for 1997-98), but between 1999 and 2003 his main professional association was with the fiercely antiregulatory National Legal Center for the Public Interest. As a judge he's written that the Endangered Species Act should not apply to a California toad because it doesn't cross state lines–a view of federal authority so extreme it would prohibit the EPA from getting involved in purely local landfills or chemical dumps.

Is Roberts's confirmation a foregone conclusion? There are still several weeks before hearings and a likely Senate vote, and his would not be the first nomination to take an unexpected turn. At this point in 1991 the Clarence Thomas nomination seemed unassailable, and in 1986 few seriously believed that Robert Bork would go down to defeat. Roberts's record and his biography may yet reveal additional troubling details.

Is it worth expending energy, emotion and money to oppose Roberts? Let's return to Ansche Hedgepeth and her french fry arrest. It may seem absurd to suggest that such a trivial case disqualifies a judge from a seat on the Supreme Court. Yet Roberts, in that case as in others, embraces a quietly authoritarian vision of social control that should raise alarm bells on both the right and the left. Managing to wring out of the law any vestige of sensible, pragmatic humanity, Roberts saw instead only the imperative to maintain ideological consistency. This is not "compassionate conservatism." If "advise and consent" means anything, it is that senators and the constituencies that agitate behind them have every reason to oppose a lifetime Supreme Court appointment for that kind of chill heart.

The Case Against Alito

Editorial
January 23, 2006

With Judge Samuel Alito, the Senate Judiciary Committee faces its most consequential Supreme Court confirmation hearing in a generation. Not since Robert Bork has the Senate encountered a nominee whose long record and fully articulated views so consistently challenge decades of progress on privacy, civil rights and control of corporations. And never in memory has a single nomination so threatened to redirect the Court as Alito's, which would replace the pragmatically conservative swing-voter Sandra Day O'Connor. Alito's opening statement before the Judiciary Committee is January 9, but his true testimony consists of fifteen years of rulings on issues from abortion to school prayer to immigration. That record demonstrates that Alito is at odds with the interests of ordinary Americans.

Supreme Court nominees get, and usually deserve, much benefit of the doubt. But with Alito, the doubt is all of the nominee's making, and has only grown with revelations of his Reagan-era memos. As an ambitious Reagan Administration lawyer, he boasted in a now-famous 1985 job application of his conviction that *Roe v. Wade* should be overturned; opposed the historic one-person, one-vote decision of the Warren Court; and waved like a badge of honor his membership in a far-right Princeton alumni network notorious for its hostility to admitting women and African-Americans. Alito's defense of Nixon-era officials implicated in illegal wiretaps makes clear–in light of today's NSA wiretap scandal–that the Bush Administration's motives in Alito's nomination extend well beyond a token nod to social conservatives.

Nothing in Alito's hundreds of federal appeals court rulings in the years since suggests any mellowing of those fundamental commitments. After a careful study, University of Chicago law professor Cass Sunstein described Alito's record of appeals court dissents as "stunning. Ninety-one percent of Alito's dissents take positions more conservative than his colleagues ... including colleagues appointed by Presidents Bush and Reagan." A new study by the Alliance for Justice makes the case even more emphatically: In so-called split decisions–the most difficult cases, which divided the appeals court–"Alito has frequently gone to the right of even his Republican-appointed colleagues to find against individuals claiming that government officials or corporations violated the law." He has argued strenuously in favor of the strip search of a 10-year-old girl not accused of criminal wrongdoing; supported warrantless surveillance of a criminal suspect when other courts had disallowed the practice; and tried to strip his fellow judges of the power to grant habeas corpus rights to undocumented immigrants, a position pointedly repudiated by the Supreme Court.

This is big-government jurisprudence with a vengeance. The only exception to Alito's big-government activism comes with the regulation of business. There he seems to be on a one-man crusade to undo decades of regulation, most clearly displayed in a still-astounding dissent arguing that the federal ban on machine guns violates the Constitution's commerce clause–a radical position (exceeding even Chief Justice John Roberts's famously constricted view of the Endangered Species Act) that would shred not only gun-control statutes but a host of environmental laws and other Congressional action.

Democrats as well as moderate Republicans have so far played their cards close. Will the handful of Democratic progressives who voted for the confirmation of Roberts–including Russell Feingold and Patrick Leahy–see themselves as free to oppose a nominee without Roberts's discretion about his own commitments? Will the party discipline so often exercised by minority leader Harry Reid extend to what is certain to be an emotional confirmation fight? Will civil-libertarian Republicans like Arlen Specter recognize in Alito not just a threat to *Roe v. Wade* but to the fundamental balance of executive and legislative power? And what about the "Gang of 14," the Republican and Democratic senators like Joe Lieberman and John McCain who last year agreed to avoid judicial filibusters except in rare circumstances? They should recall that a key principle uniting them then was that the White House should consult the Senate on judicial appointments; on Alito, the White House consulted no one but the extreme right.

The White House is banking on fear that if this second nominee goes down, Bush will nominate someone even worse. This argument ignores history: When in 1969-70 President Nixon nominated and lost both Clement Haynsworth and Harrold

Carswell, the result was not "someone worse" but the pragmatic, humane Judge Harry Blackmun, who later wrote *Roe v. Wade*; when Bork was Borked, his replacement was Anthony Kennedy, who in 1992 joined fellow Reagan nominee O'Connor to reaffirm *Roe*. Alito defeatism also ignores today's political climate: As the midterm elections draw closer, as the Iraq War scandals deepen, Senate Republicans are falling over one another to distance themselves from the Administration and the far right.

Alito will undoubtedly try to backpedal from his unambiguous track record. That only makes more urgent the case against the real Alito revealed in his memos and rulings. The American people are not ready for a nominee so profoundly committed to intrusive government, whether that means right-to-lifers intruding on sexual privacy, religious fanatics intruding in the science classroom or the NSA intruding on phone calls without a warrant. Far from being a mainstream conservative, Judge Alito represents a malignant future; his entire biography suggests he will swing the Supreme Court toward a right-wing authoritarianism that's out of step with the public and the Constitution.

Corpus Ex Machina

Patricia J. Williams
February 15, 2010

In 1976 the Supreme Court held in *Buckley v. Valeo* that the expenditure of money is a form of speech protected by the First Amendment. The implications of that case came to an absurd and unfortunate head with the January 21, 2010, decision in *Citizens United v. Federal Election Commission*. While the *Buckley* case allowed individuals unlimited spending in pursuit of political ends, *Citizens United* allows corporations that very same grace, and then some.

It is a strange moment in jurisprudence. On the one hand, corporations frequently restrict the expressions of employees or others within their purview: what they may wear, what their T-shirts may say, what political messages they may post on the walls of their cubicles. On the other, the inanimate entity of the corporation itself will now enjoy a range of First Amendment benefits not limited by principles of debate or substance, and it will be constrained only by the size of its treasury in deploying whatever technological bullhorn has the greatest chance of drowning out everyone else.

Hence, the questions on many minds are why "freedom" (as in speech) has become the functional equivalent of "expenditure" (as in money) and why on earth corporations are considered "persons" to begin with.

First, the *Buckley* decision has always been controversial, though until now it has been interpreted as allowing expenditures as a subcategory of the expressive power of living individuals only. A corporation, by contrast, is not only not human, it is property. A corporation has no natural life span, it does not vote and many are multinational. Corporations, even nonprofits, are necessarily exclusionary–their very existence premised on bottom-line calculations, competitive power grabs, branding and prospecting for self-promotion. A corporation is obliged by its bylaws to pursue its stated purpose and no other. It doesn't change its nonexistent mind or respond with compassion or feel empathy. Thus, the "corporate citizenship" that the majority in *Citizens United* touts so blithely is a very different beast from citizenship founded on a constitution of enfranchised individuals and premised on a constituency of souls united in allegiance to an ideal of community, an egalitarianism of society, the mutual shelter of a nation.

Second, a word about the history of legal "persons": for more than a hundred years, certain inanimate entities have been granted the status of fictive personhood for limited purposes. The concept grew out of the necessity for businesses to negotiate as well as to be accountable in the marketplace. When, for example, a company manufactures a defective product and sells it to you, you sue the company–not the individual executives or employees (unless there has been some act of extreme wrongdoing on their part). In other words, the company is a kind of juridical stand-in for a person, with that status rooted in the efficiency interests of contract and property law.

It takes either the most simple-minded or the most cynical state of mind to conclude from this basis that corporations are entitled to the same panoply of civil and dignitary rights as actual, fully endowed people (as in, "We, the ..."). The *Citizens United* opinion begs the question: for whom is our Bill of Rights? Is a corporation really a "who" or a "whom"? If a public "person" is capacious enough to encompass a privatized "corporate" plurality, then are "We, the people" not thereby reduced by propertied fiefdoms huddled behind a facade of "free" republicanism? If, once upon a time, enfranchisement was calculated according to such diminishing metrics as "three-fifths of a person," does not this ruling confer a similar, if magnifying, mathematical disproportion upon the organizational prostheses we know as corporations?

In 1935 the great legal realist philosopher Felix S. Cohen wrote a wonderfully illuminating article called "Transcendental Nonsense," in which he debunked (at least for that generation) the notion of corporations as persons. Cohen challenged the reasoning of the Court of Appeals of New York when it asked "Where is the corporation?" in a decision about the proper venue for a suit lodged in the State of New York against the Susquehanna Coal Company, a Pennsylvania corporation. "Nobody has ever seen a corporation," Cohen pointed out. "What right have we to believe in corporations if we don't believe in angels? To be sure, some of us have seen corporate funds, corporate transactions, etc. (just as some of us have seen angelic deeds, angelic countenances, etc.). But this does not give us the right ... to assume that it travels about from State to State as mortal men travel."

Cohen denounced such thinking as essentially "supernatural." He reminded jurists that a corporation does not really have a body with only one fixed head–that it may have a corps of employees in multiple states simultaneously. "When the vivid fictions and metaphors of traditional jurisprudence are thought of as reasons for decisions, rather than poetical or mnemonic devices for formulating decisions reached on other grounds, then the author, as well as the reader, of the opinion or argument, is apt to forget the social forces which mold the law and the social ideals by which the law is to be judged," he wrote.

In *Citizens United*, the Roberts Court has deployed just such a delusionary poetic device: "prosopopoeia," or a figure of speech that bestows upon an abstract entity the power of speech. Mssrs. Snap, Crackle and Pop, for example. The Geico gecko. The constructive endowment of speech unto such unendowed figurations is a common imaginative enterprise of the human mind. But the transference of such expressive power is always driven by, and must always be recognized as, a fiction in service to some very specific nonimaginary end. If there is no such grounding in practical purpose, we humanize a golem. We think Mr. Clean is addressing us in real time. We hallucinate.

Citizens United and the Corporate Court

Jamie Raskin
October 8, 2012

We live in what will surely come to be called the *Citizens United* era, a period in which a runaway corporatist ideology has overtaken Supreme Court jurisprudence. No longer content just to pick a president, as five conservative Republicans on the Rehnquist Court did in 2000, five conservative Republicans on the Roberts Court a decade later voted to tilt the nation's entire political process toward the views of moneyed corporate power.

In *Citizens United* (2010), the Court held that private corporations, which are nowhere mentioned in the Constitution and are not political membership organizations, enjoy the same political free speech rights as people under the First Amendment and may draw on the wealth of their treasuries to spend unlimited sums promoting or disparaging candidates for public office. The billions of dollars thus turned loose for campaign purposes at the direction of corporate managers not only can be but—under the terms of corporate law—*must* be spent to increase profits. If businesses choose to exercise their newly minted political "money speech" rights, they must work to install officials who will act as corporate tools.

The Court, transformed by the addition of Chief Justice Roberts and Samuel Alito, who were nominated by that lucky winner in *Bush v. Gore*, took this giant step to the right of all prior Courts without even being asked to do so. The petitioner, Citizens United, sought only a ruling that the electioneering provisions of the Bipartisan Campaign Reform Act (better known as McCain-Feingold) didn't apply to its on-demand movie about Hillary Clinton. But the conservatives sent the parties back to brief and argue the paradigm-shifting constitutional question they were so keen to decide. As dissenting Justice John Paul Stevens observed, the justices in the majority "changed the case to give themselves an opportunity to change the law."

Before *Citizens United* came down, corporations were already spending billions of dollars lobbying, running "issue ads," launching political action committees and soliciting PAC contributions. Moreover, CEOs, top executives and board directors—the people whose income and wealth have soared over the past several decades in relation to the rest of America—have always contributed robustly to candidates. But there was one crucial thing that CEOs could not do before *Citizens United*: reach into their corporate treasuries to bankroll campaigns promoting or opposing the election of candidates for Congress or president. This prohibition essentially established a wall of separation—not especially thick or tall, but a wall nonetheless—between corporate treasury wealth and campaigns for federal office.

The Roberts Court's 5-4 decision to demolish most of this wall also bulldozed the foundational understanding of the corporation that had governed American law for two centuries. The Court had always regarded the corporation not as a citizen with constitutional rights but as an "artificial entity" chartered by the states and endowed with extraordinary privileges in order to serve society's economic purposes. The great conservative Chief Justice John Marshall wrote in *Dartmouth College v. Woodward* (1819), "A corporation is an artificial being, invisible, intangible, and existing only in contemplation of law. Being the mere creature of law, it possesses only those properties which the charter of creation confers upon it, either expressly, or as incidental to its very existence."

This "artificial entity" understanding of corporate law prevailed until Big Tobacco lawyer and corporate-state visionary Lewis Powell, of Richmond, Virginia, joined the Court. In *First National Bank of Boston v. Bellotti* (1978), the key forerunner to *Citizens United*, Powell assembled a bare majority to give corporations and banks the right to spend without limit to influence public opinion in ballot issue campaigns. The decision, which approved the desire of banks in Massachusetts to campaign against progressive tax measures, unveiled the key doctrinal move of what would later become the *Citizens United* era: "If the speakers here were not corporations, no one would suggest that the State could silence their proposed speech," Justice Powell wrote. "The inherent worth of the speech in terms of its capacity for informing the public does not depend upon the identity of its source."

The *Bellotti* decision cracked open the door of campaign finance law, and the *Citizens United* majority blew that door off its hinges. The Court announced that, when it comes to campaign spending rights, the "identity of the speaker" is irrelevant and an impermissible basis upon which to repress the flow of money speech. What matters is the "speech" itself, never the speaker—a doctrine that would have come in handy for the public employees, public school students, whistleblowers, prisoners and minor-party candidates whose free-speech rights have been crushed by the conservative Court because of their identity as (disfavored) speakers.

Taken seriously, the *Citizens United* doctrine has astonishing implications for campaign finance. If it's true that the "identity of the speaker" is irrelevant, the City of New York—a municipal corporation, after all—should have a right to spend money telling residents for whom to vote in mayoral races. Maryland could spend tax dollars urging citizens to vote for marriage equality in November, and President Obama could order the Government Printing Office to produce a book advocating his re-election. Surely the Supreme Court would never ban a book containing campaign speech!

Further, under the new doctrine, churches—religious corporations—would have a First Amendment right not only to promote candidates from the pulpit but to spend freely on television ads advocating their election or trashing their opponents. The claim that churches surrender their right to engage in electioneering when they accept 501(c)(3) status is obsolete after *Citizens United*, which rejected the view that groups can be divested of their right to participate in politics when they receive incorporated status and special legal and financial privileges. If the identity of the speaker is truly irrelevant, there should be nothing to stop the Church of Latter-Day Saints or Harvard University from bankrolling political campaigns.

In the real world, the claim that the identity of the speaker is irrelevant cannot be taken seriously, and it is already being disregarded by the justices who signed on to it. The Court has so far declined to strike down the ban on foreign spending in American politics and the century-old ban on direct corporate contributions to candidates, laws that the new doctrine logically should invalidate. A total wipeout of campaign finance law appears to be just a step too far—at least right now—for a Court already facing plummeting public legitimacy.

But even if this incoherent doctrine goes no further, the surging stream of corporate and billionaire spending has already made a sweet difference for the Republican Party, which despairs of the nation's demographic and cultural changes and depends on a mix of right-wing propaganda and voter suppression to confuse and shrink the electorate. Indeed, the potency of *Citizens United* became clear in the same year the decision was released.

The 2010 election should have been framed by three recent corporate catastrophes: the BP oil spill in the Gulf of Mexico, which inflicted billions of dollars in damage; Massey Energy's collapsing coal mines in West Virginia, which cost twenty-nine people their lives and were enabled by the corporation's aggressive lobbying and corruption of government; and the subprime mortgage meltdown brought on by the misconduct and power plays of AIG and Wall Street, which cost the American people trillions of dollars in lost homes and home values, ravaged pension and retirement funds, and destroyed stock equity.

But the infusion into the campaign of hundreds of millions of dollars from corporate and personal sources through secretive

501(c)(4) advocacy groups, 501(c)(6) trade associations and eighty-three new Super PACs completely changed the subject. The theme of the propaganda-soaked campaign became, remarkably, the urgent importance of deregulating corporations. The Republicans and the Koch brothers–funded Tea Party captured control of the House, bringing near paralysis to the government.

Citizens United did not accomplish this feat alone; it had a junior partner in *SpeechNow.org v. FEC*. This decision came from the US Court of Appeals for the DC Circuit, which struck down limits on what individuals can give to independent expenditure campaigns, a ruling that turbo-charged the Super PACs.

Today there are 844 Super PACs and countless 501(c) vehicles; experts say billions of dollars, much of it untraceable, will flood the 2012 election. We will never know for sure whose money is paying for the show, because the front groups easily conceal their donors, including foreign corporations. Moreover, right-wing lawyers are now challenging campaign finance disclosure requirements as unconstitutional compelled speech, like making Jehovah's Witness schoolchildren pledge allegiance to the flag. They argue that corporations should be free to keep their political spending secret because they may face intimidation and even—God forbid—boycotts from consumers who dislike their politics. In other words, corporations have a right to speak because they are like people, but they should be completely insulated from the speech reactions of natural people. This is some "marketplace of ideas" the champions of corporate power have in mind for us.

Support for a constitutional amendment to reverse *Citizens United* is growing because, as Justice Stevens objected, "A democracy cannot function effectively when its constituent members believe laws are being bought and sold." An amendment to allow for reasonable regulation of campaign expenditures and contributions would empower Congress to return corporations to the economic sphere. It would also solidify the public's interest in campaign disclosure and, as Harvard professor Laurence Tribe has observed, the much-eroded interest in building a public financing system that makes participating candidates at least minimally competitive with privately financed candidates. This is an interest that the Roberts Court has trashed, in cases like *Davis v. FEC* (2008) and *Arizona Free Enterprise Club's Freedom Club PAC v. Bennett* (2011). In these decisions, the Court, in essence, ruled that privately financed candidates backed by wealthy interests not only have a right to spend to the heavens to win office but also a right, in states with public financing laws, to lock in their massive financial advantage over publicly financed candidates, whose campaign speech may not be even modestly amplified by public funding when they get outspent. Here, as distorted beyond recognition by the Roberts Court, the First Amendment becomes not the guardian of democratic discussion but the guarantee of unequal protection for well-born and wealth-backed politicians. Today, corporations can saturate the airwaves and billionaires can spend to their hearts' content, but government cannot create even a modest megaphone to help poorer candidates be heard.

A constitutional amendment to correct these distortions may seem impossible now, but all amendments seem impossible until they become inevitable. Most amendments since the Bill of Rights have expanded democracy or, like the Twenty-Fourth Amendment banning poll taxes, removed obstacles to democracy authorized by the Supreme Court. President Obama's recent statement of support for mobilizing a campaign to amend the Constitution suggests a coming surge of political engagement on the issue.

Defenders of our new plutocracy point out that there are many thousands of corporations in America, most of them small, but this bit of faux small-business populism is an irrelevant distraction from how the corporate "wealth primary" works in the real world. Major industries that have an "extractive" character and a parasitic relationship with government—Wall Street, Big Oil, Big Pharma, the military-industrial complex—have cultivated a pervasive financial dependency on elected officials that permits them to continue the exploitative symbiosis that economists call "rent-seeking." Avoiding the hazardous risks of innovation, investment and competition, many conglomerates prefer playing power politics in Washington. They don't increase the pie; they just grab ever larger slices of it.

These arrangements operate on a simple return-on-investment basis: corporations devote millions to electing and lobbying politicians and then collect hundreds of millions in tax breaks, corporate welfare, sweetheart contracts, bailouts, deregulation and inside deals. This squalid form of "public policy," which even Republicans call "crony capitalism" (in the primaries anyway), works splendidly for those involved but dismally for everyone else, including businesses that lack the finance capital to invest in the political system. A plutocratic state denies us both political justice and a fair economy.

When a bristling Justice Antonin Scalia went on CNN in July and defended *Citizens United*, which is considered a recipe for corruption by nearly 70 percent of Americans, he enlisted everyone's favorite founder. "I think Thomas Jefferson would have said, 'The more speech, the better,'" Scalia opined.

One must charitably assume Scalia's utter ignorance of Jefferson's political philosophy and how much the Sage of Monticello feared the rise of a "single and splendid government of an aristocracy, founded on banking institutions, and moneyed incorporations," which he foresaw "riding and ruling over the plundered ploughmen and beggared yeomanry." The *Citizens United* era bears a disturbing resemblance to Jefferson's nightmare vision of what might happen if corporate power swallowed the government.

A New Strategy for Voting Rights

Ari Berman
July 3, 2013

Hank Sanders grew up in segregated, rural southern Alabama and in 1971 moved to Selma—the birthplace of the Voting Rights Act. Before the VRA, only 393 of the 15,000 black voting-age residents in Dallas County, where Selma is located, were registered to vote. Less than a year later, after federal registrars arrived in August 1965, more than 10,000 black voters had been added to the rolls. Sanders experienced first-hand how the VRA transformed Selma and the rest of the country. In 1983, he became the first African-American state senator from the Alabama Black Belt since Reconstruction, representing a new majority-black district created by the VRA.

Thirty years later, Sanders watched in disbelief this June as the Supreme Court overturned the centerpiece of the VRA in *Shelby County v. Holder*. "It's the most destructive Supreme Court decision in my lifetime," Sanders said. "It reverses the very foundation of all the progress that we have made." Reactions in Selma, he said, "ranged from shock to resignation."

The Court's conservative majority struck down Section 4 of the law, which determines how states are covered under Section 5— the vital provision that requires states with the worst history of racial discrimination in voting, dating back to the 1960s and '70s, to clear electoral changes with the federal government. Without Section 4, there's no Section 5. The most effective provision of the country's most important civil rights law is now a ghost unless Congress resurrects it.

"We have no power under the Constitution to invalidate this democratically adopted legislation," Justice Antonin Scalia wrote in his dissent on the Defense of Marriage Act. Yet that reasoning didn't stop Scalia and Chief Justice John Roberts from gutting the VRA, which has been overwhelmingly reauthorized four times by Congress (1970, 1975, 1982, 2006) and signed by four Republican presidents (Nixon, Ford, Reagan, Bush). "The Voting Rights Act became one of the most consequential, efficacious, and amply justified exercises of federal legislative power in our Nation's history," Justice Ruth Bader Ginsburg wrote in her fiery dissent.

The Roberts majority struck down Section 4 for violating the "'fundamental principle of equal sovereignty' among the States," an argument with roots in Southern segregationist opposition to Reconstruction. (In a biting rebuke, Judge Richard Posner, the pre-eminent legal theorist at the University of Chicago, wrote that "there is no such principle" of constitutional law and that "the opinion rests on air.") The Roberts decision ignored 250 years of slavery in America, nearly 100 years of Jim Crow and fifty years of persistent attempts to subvert the VRA. The Justice Department blocked 1,116 discriminatory voting changes from taking effect under Section 5 from 1965 to 2004 and objected to thirty-seven electoral proposals after Congress reauthorized the law in 2006. "The Supreme Court didn't recognize the degree to which voter suppression is still a problem around the country," President Obama, visiting Senegal, said following the decision.

Freed from Section 5, the states of the Old Confederacy will dust off the pre-1965 playbook, passing onerous new voting restrictions that can be challenged only through a preliminary injunction or after years of lengthy litigation, often in hostile Southern courts, with the burden of proof now on those facing discrimination rather than on those who discriminate. "Without Section 5, all kinds of things will be passed to limit the right to vote," says Sanders. "I can't anticipate all the creativity we will run into." Immediately after the decision, five Southern states—Alabama, Mississippi, South Carolina, Texas and Virginia—rushed to implement new voter-ID laws that disproportionately affect young and minority voters. Voting changes found to be discriminatory by a federal court last year—like the Texas voter-ID law—will go into effect. ("Eric Holder can no longer deny #VoterID in #Texas," Texas Attorney General Greg Abbott tweeted the morning of the decision.) Beyond voter ID, states like North Carolina are close to drastically cutting early voting and eliminating same-day registration. According to the Advancement Project, a Washington civil rights organization, "Eleven out of the 15 states covered by Section 5 enacted, or are pursuing, restrictive voting laws this year."

Judith Browne-Dianis, Advancement Project co-director, says voting rights groups have developed a four-pronged strategy to counteract the decision: challenge new voting restrictions through preliminary injunctions and Section 2 of the VRA (which applies nationwide, but puts the onus on plaintiffs to prove that a law is discriminatory after enactment); pressure Congress to reconstruct the VRA; draft a new coverage formula for Section 4; and mobilize indignant voters to make their voices heard, starting with the fiftieth anniversary of the March on Washington on August 28. "All of those pieces have to happen at the same time," she says.

On the night of the decision, the NAACP held a conference call with its 1,200 local chapters to prepare them for the tough fight ahead. A few days later, 18,000 people joined a conference call with a broad array of democratic reform and civil rights groups to discuss the post–*Shelby County* strategy. "We've got to move from outrage to action," says Jotaka Eaddy, senior director of voting rights at the NAACP. "It's important that people know there's an attack on voting rights. It's even more important that people know they can do something about it."

The thorniest issue is what a revised Section 4 should look like, which Spencer Overton, professor of law at George Washington University Law School, calls a "political Rubik's Cube." A consensus has not yet emerged. Overton believes the best fix is to cover states based on recent Section 2 and Section 5 violations in the past two to five years, and to more easily "bail in" states with bad records under Section 3 of the VRA. "We certainly want this to be appropriately tailored, recognizing that it will be challenged in the future," Overton says. He also thinks Congress should make jurisdictions disclose voting changes online to show they're not discriminatory and bolster the ability of voting rights groups and the Justice Department to win preliminary injunctions.

It remains to be seen whether a Congress that can scarcely do more than name post offices is capable of rewriting the country's most important civil rights law. The chairs of the Senate and House Judiciary committees have pledged to hold hearings soon, and prominent Republicans like James Sensenbrenner, Eric Cantor and Chuck Grassley have expressed openness to a legislative fix. The GOP caucus is whiter, more conservative and more Southern than it was during the last reauthorization, although opposition to a new VRA could prove disastrous for a party now embarking, at least rhetorically, on a well-publicized "rebranding." Nancy Pelosi has suggested a name for the new law, after the man who nearly died marching in Selma for voting rights: the John Lewis Voting Rights Act.

The VRA decision could produce a significant backlash among minority voters, just as the voter suppression attempts of 2012 spurred black turnout, which surpassed white turnout for the first time in US history. In much the same way that the VRA's passage in 1965 spurred counter-mobilization drives by the likes of George Wallace, which registered hundreds of thousands of conservative white voters in the 1960s, so too could the loss of Section 5 motivate a new wave of minority voting activism. "The election of 2012 put voting rights back on the map, because people saw the extent to which politicians would go to suppress the vote," says Browne-Dianis. "This decision is going to take it to the next level. People now get that it's not only these state legislatures, but it's the courts that are rolling back voting rights. Many people feel like, 'It's not going to happen on our watch.'"

The Roberts Court Tunes In to Democracy, for Once

David Cole
July 2, 2015

On back-to-back days at the end of its term, the Supreme Court sustained Obamacare against (another) Tea Party challenge and extended the constitutional freedom to marry to same-sex couples nationwide. Thanks to the Roberts Court, millions of working-poor and middle-income people won't lose their health insurance, and millions of gay and lesbian Americans will have the right to marry. But this is the same Court that has sharply restricted affirmative action, invalidated a critical section of the Voting Rights Act, freed corporations to spend unlimited amounts of money on political campaigns, and allowed businesses to compel arbitration in contracts that effectively precludes all remedies for illegal discrimination. So what happened this time?

The simple answer in both instances is Justice Anthony Kennedy, who is the decisive vote so often that we really should call it the Kennedy Court.

Kennedy was the swing vote on same-sex marriage, and in the Obamacare decision, Chief Justice John Roberts joined him in siding with the liberals. The dissenters in both cases excoriated their conservative friends not only for deserting them, but also for abandoning the proper judicial role. In Antonin Scalia's view, the Court in *King v. Burwell* (the Obamacare case) impermissibly rewrote the statute—so much so that from now on, the justice opined, the law ought to be called "SCOTUScare." In *Obergefell v. Hodges* (the marriage decision), Roberts's dissent accused Kennedy and the majority of "an act of will, not legal judgment," while Scalia railed against the "hubris reflected in today's judicial Putsch."

In fact, both decisions reflect a Court (or at least a majority) that is highly attuned to its responsibility in a democracy. In the Obamacare case, the challengers had sought to enlist the Court in a game of "gotcha" with Congress, fixing on four words—"established by the State"—found in an obscure subsection of a 900-page statute and urging the Court to adopt an interpretation that would have heralded the law's demise. They argued that the four words should preclude tax credits for anyone in the 34 states that are serviced by a federally administered insurance exchange. This reading would have rendered meaningless several other provisions in the statute, made the federal exchanges unworkable, and altogether doomed local insurance markets, which require the broad participation of healthy individuals, made possible through tax credits. Respecting Congress's decision to enact the law, the Court properly allowed it to function as the lawmakers plainly intended.

The marriage decision is different. Here, the question was whether the Court would recognize a new constitutional right and require the states to afford same-sex couples the right to marry. It was little surprise that Kennedy wrote the decision: He has now written every major gay-rights ruling that the Court has made over the last 20 years—striking down first a Colorado referendum barring the protection of gays and lesbians under anti-discrimination codes; then a Texas law making homosexual sodomy a crime; then, last year, the federal Defense of Marriage Act.

Kennedy reasoned that the right to marry is a fundamental one, and that the reasons we protect it apply equally to same-sex couples. For straight and gay alike, he wrote, marriage furthers personal autonomy, intimate association, and child rearing, and is "a keystone of our social order." As a result, there is no good reason to deny same-sex couples equal access to marriage.

The decision rested primarily on the Constitution's due-process clause, which the Court has previously interpreted to protect the rights of contraception, sexual intimacy, abortion, and the marriage rights of interracial couples, prisoners, and fathers behind on their child-custody payments. Kennedy also relied on the equal-protection clause, ruling that the state had advanced no compelling reason to treat gay and straight couples differently with regard to marriage.

The dissenters charged the majority with having unilaterally redefined marriage, abandoning the framers' original intent and imposing their own views of morality on the nation. But these criticisms are overwrought. The definition of marriage was precisely at issue in the case. If original intent still controlled constitutional law, racial segregation and sex discrimination would be valid today. And the Court did not impose its own views of morality, but rather its own best reading of a constitutional tradition that has for decades recognized protection for marriage and associated intimate, private rights.

But most important, the Court did not invent the right to same-sex marriage through an act of pure will. *Obergefell* was the capstone of a more than two-decades-long struggle by people committed to a vision of equality. When that struggle began, the idea of same-sex marriage was an oxymoron; by the time the Court took up the question, it had become an inevitability. That change came about not through the whim of five justices, but through the painstaking work of thousands of people across the country committed to an idea of equality—and willing to fight for it in state legislatures and courts, on state referendums, in their churches and their communities. And that is just how constitutional law has generally evolved in our society: through the persistent struggle of groups of committed citizens.

Chief Justice Roberts closed his dissent in *Obergefell* by acknowledging that many would celebrate the decision, but that they should "not celebrate the Constitution. It had nothing to do with it." He's wrong. If constitutional law is understood as an evolving doctrine rather than the dead hand of the past, we should celebrate not just the decision, but the Constitution itself—and the people who have worked so long and hard to make constitutional law reflect our deepest commitments to equal dignity for all.

PART FIVE
Takeover

Supreme Court Showdown

Nan Aron and Kyle C. Barry
February 15, 2016

Once again, Justice Antonin Scalia is in the middle of a presidential election. Fifteen years ago, in December 2000, he was a part of the 5-4 Supreme Court majority in *Bush v. Gore* that halted the Florida recount and handed the election to Republican George W. Bush. The much-maligned decision is a regrettable example of the Court placing politics above the law, with five Republican-appointed justices ignoring constitutional principles to propel a new Republican president into office. In later years, Justice Scalia's defense of the case boiled down to, "Get over it!"

On February 13, Scalia, ever brilliant, witty, and unrepentant, died at the age of 79. His death creates a vacancy on a closely divided Court that decides, often by a single vote, some of the nation's most pressing issues. The vacancy comes as the Supreme Court is poised to decide a litany of blockbuster cases—abortion, affirmative action, labor, religious freedom, healthcare, voting rights, and the death penalty are all before the Court. It also thrusts the Supreme Court to the forefront of the 2016 election. The Court has always been the most important issue of this election—Scalia was not the oldest member of the Court, and three more justices will be in their 80s during the next president's term. But with Scalia's death, a once esoteric issue that has struggled for airtime became immediate and tangible. The impact was swift, with the Supreme Court the first subject raised during the Republican debate in South Carolina on the night of Scalia's death.

Throughout a 30-year tenure that spanned five presidents, Scalia anchored the Court's conservative wing.

Scalia is the first Supreme Court Justice to die mid-term since Robert Jackson in 1954, and losing him hurts the conservative special interests who have angled for big victories this year. Throughout a 30-year tenure that spanned five presidents, Scalia anchored the Court's conservative wing, not just as a reliable vote, but as a legal movement's intellectual leader who awed popular audiences with breezy, quotable opinions that persuaded through humor and biting criticism. Without Scalia, the current Court's 5-4 conservative majority is gone, and many of the most contentious cases will result in either a 4-4 tie or a 5-3 decision with Justice Anthony Kennedy joining the more liberal justices, as he did last year on same-sex marriage.

In a tie, the Court simply affirms the lower court, and the result is as if the Court never heard the case at all. That's a problem for the special interests that have engineered aggressive legal challenges designed specifically for the Supreme Court to decide. That strategy has worked to great effect over the past decade. Time and again, the Court's conservatives have advanced a pro-corporate, right-wing agenda by doing things that lower courts are unable or unwilling to do: Overturning well-established precedent, unilaterally changing questions before the Court, deciding issues about which there is no real dispute—all have become the keys to conservative success in the Supreme Court.

Several pending cases reflect that strategy. In *Friedrichs v. California Teachers Association*, the case designed to defund the labor movement, the plaintiffs intentionally lost in the lower courts so they could ask the Supreme Court to overturn its own unanimous precedent from 1977. In *Evenwel v. Abbott*, a challenge to equal voting rights under the Court's "one person, one vote" doctrine, the lower court observed that the plaintiffs are "relying upon a theory never before accepted by the Supreme Court or any circuit court." And to decide whether the Affordable Care Act's birth-control mandate violates the rights of religious organizations, the Court consolidated seven appeals, not one of which blocked the mandate (the Eighth Circuit disagreed, but that decision isn't before the Court). Across these issues—labor, voting rights, women's health—the plaintiffs were counting on Justice Scalia and the Court's conservatives. The lower courts were never the end game, and a potential 4-4 split was never the plan.

Justice Scalia was an adherent of originalism, the judicial philosophy focused on the original meaning of legal texts without regard to evolving social norms. A central tenet is that judges should not be concerned with outcomes; rather, they must faithfully apply legal texts according to their original understanding, and follow the text to whatever result it leads. At bottom, originalism requires fidelity to legal obligation over desired policy. Scalia loudly proselytized the theory, winning converts among conservative lawyers and politicians alike, even if, as in cases like *Bush v. Gore*, he contravened his own principles.

And yet in response to his death, Scalia's fellow Republicans in the Senate quickly dismissed constitutional obligation—both the president's to name a successor and their own to provide advice and consent—in favor of keeping the seat open beyond the election. Even without a nominee to oppose, the Senate's Republican leadership, including majority leader Mitch McConnell and Judiciary Committee chairman Chuck Grassley, have said that President Obama, who has more than 300 days left in office, shouldn't appoint Scalia's replacement. Republican Senator and presidential candidate Ted Cruz has promised to filibuster any nominee. They've cited a lack of precedent for appointing justices in election years, but in fact six Supreme Court justices have been confirmed in presidential election years since 1900, including Republican-appointee Justice Kennedy in February 1988.

Senate inaction likely means the Court will be without one justice for two terms.

What's more, Senate inaction likely means the Court will be without one justice for two terms. The next Supreme Court term will be nearly half over when the next president is sworn in, and even if that president nominates quickly, confirmation is unlikely before the term's end. That means two years of potential 4-4 deadlocks that leave the Court unable to decide major constitutional issues. Thus refusing to even vote on a nominee is not just an abdication of constitutional duty; it will manufacture a constitutional crisis.

Unfortunately, a strategy of obstruction without regard to consequence is not new. There are also 34 judicial nominees to other federal courts pending, including four to circuit courts of appeals. Yet no votes are scheduled, and this Senate is on pace to confirm the fewest judges in a two-year congress since 1951-52. Even in the minority, Republicans worked to block President Obama's judicial nominees, including in 2013, when they filibustered three nominees to the DC Circuit Court of Appeals. But a stalled Supreme Court nominee would amplify scrutiny of this obstruction, and that could pressure a Republican caucus that has 24 seats up for election in November (Democrats have just 10). Some of the Republican incumbents facing contested elections, like Ron Johnson in Wisconsin and Pat Toomey in Pennsylvania, are already under fire for blocking or delaying circuit court nominees in their home states.

Without question the Supreme Court should be at the center of this election, and a new vacancy puts it there. Americans deserve to know what kind of justices a candidate would appoint, and the 2016 elections will have an enormous impact on the Court's future. But what this election will not decide is who gets to replace Justice Scalia. That happened in 2012, when the American people elected President Obama to another four-year term that still has 11 months remaining. Once the president nominates, the Senate must take seriously its constitutional obligation to give that nominee a fair hearing and a timely vote. They owe it to Justice Scalia and his philosophy of obligation over outcome. And as stewards of our democratic institutions, they owe it to the American people.

For our part, progressives must unite around a nominee, and fight not just for a confirmation this year, but for the future of the Supreme Court. This is a rare moment to galvanize all our communities around an issue that profoundly affects every constituency, and to commit to a new vision of the Court that provides equal justice to all Americans, not just powerful special interests.

After Kavanaugh

John Nichols
October 10, 2018

With the confirmation of Brett Kavanaugh, the Supreme Court of the United States is now a wholly realized threat not just to social and economic progress, but to equal justice under the law. Kavanaugh himself promised that would be the case at the conclusion of the confirmation charade orchestrated by Senate majority leader Mitch McConnell and Senate Judiciary Committee chairman Chuck Grassley. The nominee raged against "the left" and imagined that senators who had concerns about allegations of sexual abuse, his lies under oath, and his judicial record were part of "a calculated and orchestrated political hit, fueled with apparent pent-up anger about President Trump and the 2016 election." Now that Kavanaugh has been seated, how can any of us forget the menacing message in his testimony: "What goes around comes around"?

These are more than the idle words of an out-of-control partisan. Because Kavanaugh could occupy the Court into the 2050s, they represent a chilling threat that must be addressed. If Democrats take charge of the House Judiciary Committee in November, they have a duty to examine testimony that former Supreme Court justice John Paul Stevens said rendered

Kavanaugh unfit to serve on the high court, along with credible complaints about abuse and evidence that the new justice perjured himself under oath.

It is important for progressives to hold Kavanaugh to account, but that cannot be the end of it. There is a much broader need to come to grips with the challenges posed by a fully corrupted confirmation process and a fully compromised Court. The first response must be a clear-eyed and pragmatic focus on the midterm elections, which are now just weeks away. It is easy—and appropriate—to be angry with Senator Susan Collins, the faux moderate who has never voted against a Republican nominee for the Court. Unlike the sole dissenting Republican, Senator Lisa Murkowski, who described Dr. Christine Blasey Ford's testimony as "very credible" and took seriously the message of Alaskans who said that Kavanaugh should not be confirmed, Collins provided essential cover for McConnell's machinations in a shameful floor speech praising the nominee.

Yet Collins is not on the ballot this year. Other Republican senators who aggressively defended Kavanaugh are up for reelection, and several of them—particularly Dean Heller in Nevada and Ted Cruz in Texas—are vulnerable. The focus should be on those races, and on the reelection runs of red-state Democrats who, unlike West Virginia's calculating Joe Manchin, cast votes of conscience against Trump's nominee. When the critical test came, North Dakota's Heidi Heitkamp, Missouri's Claire McCaskill, and Indiana's Joe Donnelly did the right thing. If they are reelected in November, the signal will be that standing strong against the president's bully-boy politics is morally necessary and politically smart. Wins by Democrats in these races have the potential to flip the Senate and put the people who opposed Kavanaugh in charge of the confirmation process going forward. That would be sweet justice.

Shifting control of the Senate is vital, but that's still an insufficient response; progressives must acknowledge the broader crisis and redouble their efforts to address it. Kavanaugh joins a right-wing activist majority on the Court that extends not from the will of the people but from our broken and dysfunctional politics. He is the fourth member of that majority to be nominated by a president who lost the popular vote. The genius of the American experiment has been its adaptability—much of it achieved by amending a Constitution that the founders knew would need to be changed. Yet the Electoral College lingers as the unreformed remnant of a period in which compromises between slaveholders and wealthy merchants were designed to thwart democracy. Advocates for constitutional amendments to get corporate money out of politics and to guarantee the right to vote—essential responses to the Court's disastrous decisions in *Citizens United v. FEC* and *Shelby County v. Holder*—must add to their agenda the elimination of the Electoral College. They can also work for short-term fixes like the National Popular Vote Interstate Compact, in which states formally agree to cast their electoral votes for the winner of the popular ballot.

Progressives must also make structural reform of the courts a priority. A century ago, presidential contenders like Theodore Roosevelt and Robert La Follette proposed sweeping reforms of the federal judiciary, which was well understood as a reactionary

threat. There were calls for legislation and constitutional amendments that would give Congress the power to defend laws that
the Supreme Court sought to overturn, and to change the courts
themselves with term limits for judges and provisions for the
recall of errant jurists. President Franklin Roosevelt tried in the
1930s to expand the Supreme Court so that dinosaur justices
appointed in the distant past could not block the New Deal.
These calls for reform were dismissed as radical. But history
often reminds us that the radicalism of one moment is the common sense of the next. That next moment has come. The awful
corruptions of politics and process that put Brett Kavanaugh on
the Supreme Court demand the immediate response of a new
Senate and the longer-term response of a common-sense movement to reform the federal judiciary.

The Bosses' Constitution

Jedediah Britton-Purdy
September 12, 2018

In an unusually stinging dissent from the final major ruling of the Supreme Court's 2017–18 term, Justice Elena Kagan accused the Court's conservative majority of "weaponizing" the First Amendment. In a string of recent decisions, she argued, these justices had turned the protection of free speech into an all-purpose tool for shredding democratic policy choices that they disliked.

The case was *Janus v. AFSCME*, and the majority had just announced that public employees could not be required to pay dues for a union's collective-bargaining representation if they had opted not to join the union. For decades, workers who didn't join a union were exempted from paying general union dues (used for organizing, political advocacy, and the like), but they were required to contribute money to those direct services, such as collective bargaining, that they had benefited from. In *Janus*, the Court ruled that such a requirement violated the First Amendment. Writing for the majority, Justice Samuel Alito contended that unions are always political: Even in collective bargaining, unions engage in political advocacy and so to pay for union services is a violation of an employee's right to free speech.

Though couched in the neutral terms of the First Amendment, the Court's ruling wasn't just about free speech; it had clear partisan implications. The decision is likely to result in a hit to union coffers, both weakening workers' power and dampening union support for Democrats and public spending. But as Kagan made clear in her dissent, the stakes were even higher. Over the last decade, the Supreme Court has used the First Amendment as a justification for slashing regulations and protecting private economic power. In 2010, the Court ruled in *Citizens United* that the First Amendment guaranteed corporations (as well as unions) the right to spend unlimited sums of money in support of political candidates. In 2011, the Court ruled that the First Amendment protected the sale of prescription data by pharmacists to drug companies, which used it to tailor their advertising to specific doctors. Invoking free speech, the Supreme Court and the lower federal courts have also struck down a series of limits on advertising for pharmaceuticals and tobacco products, including health-labeling requirements and a ban on cigarette advertising near schools. Scholars and lawyers worry that, if spending money and transferring data are forms of speech, nearly any transaction might be constitutionally protected in an economy where everything is information and everything is for sale.

Yet the weaponization of the First Amendment isn't new. *Citizens United* has become notorious, but it merely extended a principle that the Court announced back in 1976 with its decision in *Buckley v. Valeo*, a ruling that gutted Congress's post-Watergate attempts at campaign-finance reform. But what makes the weaponization of free speech by today's Court so worrisome is that it's only one part of a much broader pattern in which the Court has aimed its most aggressive jurisprudence against egalitarian redistribution and the interests of working-class Americans.

All of these rulings are part and parcel of the libertarian right's attack on the redistributive state. But there is also a larger ambition at work here: to tilt the scales of capitalist democracy by hindering the capacity of democratic politics to reshape the market and assert the equality of citizens against the vast disparities of rich and poor. In so doing, the Court has recast the Constitution's core principles of personal freedom, equality, and democratic accountability to entrench the power of employers and the wealthy. A Court that once advanced a modest but real egalitarianism by supporting desegregation, voting rights, and criminal-justice reform is now creating a Bosses' Constitution.

*

Today, it is easy to see the conservative justices as part of a Republican apparatus: a right-wing legal movement, centered on the Federalist Society and running through the White House and the offices of key senators, that groomed Alito and Chief Justice John Roberts and is now in control of the Trump administration's judicial appointments. But the roots of an anti-redistribution, market-protecting Constitution are older than today's conservative legal movement. The Bosses' Constitution emerged at the end of, and in reaction to, the three decades after World War II of widely shared growth and expanded social protections, with the flattest distributions of wealth and income the country had ever seen and a strong role for organized labor in managing and benefiting from the national economy. For the center-right, these decades of growing equality presented a threat: Wages, public spending, union power, and bureaucratic regulation were undermining profits and free enterprise. Economist-publicists like Friedrich Hayek and Milton Friedman argued vigorously for cutting back the power of unions and of government redistribution programs to preserve market discipline and the libertarian freedom to invest in businesses and to hire and fire workers. Business elites listened, along with a new generation of corporate lawyers, who have always been the single greatest power center in the legal profession.

In a 1971 memo to the US Chamber of Commerce, future Supreme Court Justice Lewis Powell—then a lawyer practicing corporate law in Virginia—captured the spirit of the decade's libertarian turn. Favorably citing Friedman and calling on American business to make a full-court press for "the preservation of the system [of free enterprise] itself," Powell adopted Hayek's signature argument that "the threat to the enterprise system ... also is a threat to individual freedom. ... Freedom as a concept is indivisible. As the experience of the socialist and totalitarian states demonstrates, the contraction and denial of economic freedom is followed inevitably by governmental restrictions on other cherished rights."

A few months later, Powell was nominated by Richard Nixon for a seat on the Supreme Court. In 1973, Powell wrote the opinion in which the Court ruled that there was no constitutional protection for the poor, and no violation of equal protection when school-funding schemes mandated wildly different levels of funding in rich and poor neighborhoods. In 1976, his fellow Nixon appointee Harry Blackmun wrote the first opinion using free speech to protect commercial advertising, setting up the Court's later rulings protecting tobacco and pharmaceutical ads from regulation. (A prescient dissent by the hardheaded conservative justice William Rehnquist conjured up a dystopia of ads pitching drugs for pain and anxiety—exactly the world we live in now, in which drug companies have fueled the opioid crisis.)

The same year that the Court ruled that commercial advertising deserved constitutional protection as speech, it also issued a per curiam (unsigned) ruling in *Buckley v. Valeo*, which held that wealthy individuals, including candidates, could spend unlimited amounts on campaign ads, and that caps on total spending by political campaigns were also unconstitutional—a decision guaranteeing that wealth would translate directly into campaign speech. In 1978, Powell wrote the first opinion in which the Court subjected affirmative action to "strict scrutiny," its most aggressive review, setting in motion the steady erosion of an imperfect but important tool for mitigating racial inequality. By the end of the decade, the Court had declared economic inequality to be constitutionally benign and commercial advertising to be protected speech, and it also ruled that the Constitution forbade many of the efforts to check economic power and racial inequality through policies like campaign-finance laws and affirmative action.

The link between Powell's memo and the Supreme Court's turn in the 1970s wasn't a conspiracy, except in the sense that all political organizing is a kind of open conspiracy. It was, however, very important ideological work. At any time in US history, the Constitution's principle concepts—liberty, equality, political accountability—have the meanings that judicial interpretation assigns to them. These interpretations—even when they're styled "originalist"—always respond to the political movements, crises, and felt imperatives of the times, as inflected by the elite lawyers who populate the Court.

This was true of the Warren Court, which left its mark on the civil-rights era by desegregating public life, guaranteeing meaningful protections for the criminally accused, and making the principle of "one person, one vote" a part of US law for the first time in history. It was true as well of the justices in the New Deal era, who offered a legal basis for a powerful regulatory state and pro-union labor law that earlier Courts had persistently undermined. And it was also true of the justices of the 1970s, who, though they might not have put it as vividly as Powell did, saw their job as protecting constitutional liberty by pushing back against the power of the state to redistribute wealth and influence.

*

This new generation of justices insisted that their project was neither partisan nor ideological, but in effect it was both. At a time when the Democrats held the House and the Senate, the goal of this jurisprudence was to prevent lawmakers from entrenching themselves and their allies in power—in particular the unions and minority groups that were key Democratic constituencies.

The way to stop this was by limiting lawmakers' power to distribute privileges, and above all to prevent whoever was in power from tilting future elections toward their preferred successors. The post-Watergate effort to get money out of politics, these justices argued, favored the parties and candidates who could muster large volunteer networks (which tended to be the Democrats and unions), and it curtailed the influence of outsiders (which tended to be businessmen and financial elites keen to get involved in politics) who used their money to break into the mix. As far as these justices were concerned, this looked like picking winners—no matter that their rulings wound up stacking the deck for the wealthy.

The justices' prescription for heading off favoritism and entrenched interests mirrored some of the core ideological commitments of democracy-skeptical libertarianism. They treated politics as if it were one more market, in which spending and advertising were simply ways of expressing arguments. The Court's opinions portrayed voters as reasoning like the idealized consumers in rational-choice theory, considering their options (with help from the ever-informative advertisers) and making the decisions that best served their interests. In a literal free marketplace of ideas, political spending would preserve (as the Court put it in *Buckley*) "a republic where the people are sovereign."

Of course, this worked mainly to the benefit of one party and not the other. And it worked even more clearly to the benefit of the wealthy, who could now leverage their economic power to influence the political "market." And that's exactly what's happened. Since the 1970s, the Supreme Court's campaign-finance decisions have helped keep wealth at the center of political influence, while its decisions on education spending, poverty, and race have helped protect the nation's growing inequality from egalitarian disruption. This jurisprudence has also made it harder for those from outside circles to run for office. Politics in America has become the province of the rich: Today, less than 2 percent of members of Congress entered politics from blue-collar jobs, and at least 50 percent, according to one estimate, are millionaires.

American politics has always been profoundly divided along class lines. Today's disproportionate representation of the wealthy amplifies this. Since 1980, we have seen substantial cuts in public higher education, a growth in income inequality, the stagnation of wages, and a halving of the top marginal tax rate. The cost of class entrenchment is a Bosses' Republic.

The influence that wealth exercises over politics is not a matter of bribes, but rather structural and social. It is structural because many lawmakers are either white-collar professionals or wealthy, and also because the high cost of political campaigns requires constant infusions of money, and politicians and their staffers cannot afford to forget who has it. It is social because, thanks to the structural intertwining of money and power, those who hold power know, listen to, care about, and identify with those who have money—that is, people like themselves.

The gap between the reality of class entrenchment and the Supreme Court's rhapsodizing about political spending as the heart of self-rule is what makes the weaponized First Amendment ideological in the worst sense. This jurisprudence actively obscures how class entrenchment in America's legislative branch poses a threat to democratic self-rule. By doing so, it also deepens the problem, both by denying the existence of the basic conflict in capitalist democracies between organized money and organized people, and by taking a side in that conflict to protect and increase money's power.

Despite the Court's high-minded ideas about letting the people rule, there is no such thing as genuine neutrality when it comes to the interaction between economic and political power. There are only various rules for relating the two, from banning all private money in elections (one extreme) to treating elections as markets (the other). The United States right now is pretty close to the second extreme.

What progressives need to formulate in response is a constitutional vision of their own that takes economic power seriously and puts democratic power first. Democratic power is the means to foster dignified, secure lives in a community of relative equals. It does this by ensuring people what they need—health care, education, shelter, work, rest—and constraining the economic power that makes them vulnerable to insecurity and deprivation.

Democratic power can achieve this only by doing precisely what the weaponized First Amendment prohibits: actively shaping the terrain of political contests, in campaigns and unions and advertising, not to silence the wealthy per se, but to put them under the same rules as everyone else. This should be part of a larger vision of constitutional equality that would strengthen the right to vote and challenge racially disparate policing and incarceration. Its heart should be the power to make democracy itself more democratic by controlling the power of wealth.

As the Court noted in 2008, "making and implementing judgments about which strengths should be permitted to contribute to the outcome of an election" is a dangerous business, but dangerous is not the same as optional. Either democratic majorities will make decisions about the basic workings of our democracy, or those decisions will be made implicitly through the translation of economic power into political power. The first tack can be risky. The second, from the point of view of democracy, can be worse.

Distribution—both of the material goods of a society and of political power—is not an issue that a capitalist democracy can somehow avoid with the right constitutional formula. The questions of who gets what and who has the power to do what will be answered one way or another, and by one group or another. Redistribution is simply the word for giving real democracy a chance against the false neutrality of the Bosses' Constitution.

FORUM: What's the Matter With the Supreme Court?

Michael Klarman, Eli Noam and Nadine Strossen, Sanford Levinson, Mark Tushnet
September 5, 2018

For nearly two months now, the Senate has been considering the president's nomination of Brett Kavanaugh—a partisan hack undistinguished but for his marked commitment to the limitlessness of executive power—as an associate justice on the Supreme Court. A painfully sad sequel to the judicial coup d'état that was last year's elevation of Neil Gorsuch to what rightfully should have been Merrick Garland's seat, Kavanaugh's confirmation now appears all but certain, presenting a clear and present danger to the rights and liberties of countless Americans—a calamity from which the country will not recover, if it does at all, for many, many years.

The problem goes beyond Kavanaugh, however, and deeper than Trump. How is it possible—and why should it be—for a proudly incompetent, boisterously corrupt president who, by any reasonable measure, lost the election by millions of votes to shape the interpretation of the Constitution by the high court for decades to come? Why is it that the fate of the republic itself hinges on the health and well-being of a single octogenarian?

Somewhere in the constitutional design of the Supreme Court something is not working—or, more frighteningly, perhaps it is working all too well.

To find out what really ails the Supreme Court, and how it can be fixed, we asked a few progressive constitutional lawyers to offer their prescriptions.

—*Richard Kreitner*

*

SIZE MATTERS

Michael Klarman

The Supreme Court has always been a political institution, but in recent decades it has become an adjunct of the Republican Party. Today's conservative majority on the Court busts labor unions (which remain the backbone of the Democratic Party) and undermines class-action litigation (which the Republican justices regard as a gravy train for plaintiffs' lawyers, who contribute disproportionately to Democratic coffers). That same majority legitimizes voter suppression to diminish turnout among racial minorities, poor people, and young adults—all to the disadvantage of the Democratic Party. Conservative justices have refused to intervene against gerrymandering, which vastly inflates Republican power at the state and national levels. These same justices have also used dubious interpretations of the First Amendment in campaign-finance rulings that inevitably redound to the benefit of the Republican Party, which derives a disproportionate share of its resources from billionaire donors. The Court's Republican majority ferrets out nonexistent animus against conservative Christians in a Colorado civil-rights commission, while turning a blind eye to transparent animus against Muslims within the Trump administration. And, lest we forget, Republican justices shut down a recount that jeopardized the prospects of their party's presidential candidate.

When progressives win back political power, they will be confronted with the most conservative Supreme Court in nearly a century. It is easy to imagine that Court concocting constitutional arguments against virtually every measure a progressive administration might pursue—for example, universal health care, a ban on assault weapons, protections for voting rights, and environmental regulations to mitigate the effects of human-caused global climate change.

The most direct solution would be to increase the institution's size. Adding one justice would be an obvious and eminently just solution to Mitch McConnell's theft of the seat President Obama nominated Merrick Garland to fill. But Democrats should not stop there. Altering the size of the Court has been done many times in American history (though not since 1870), and is clearly constitutional.

Democratic candidates have won the popular vote in six of the last seven presidential elections. One would think that would entitle Democrats to control of the Supreme Court. But such control has eluded them because of the vagaries of the Supreme Court appointments process, our absurd Electoral College system, Senator McConnell's theft of the Scalia seat, and Russian meddling in the 2016 election. A president who lost the popular election by 2.9 million votes, whose victory was rendered possible only by an FBI director's misguided intervention in the final days of the contest and by Russian meddling in the election, ought not to be making appointments to the Supreme Court that will continue to affect the country for the next 30-plus years.

Of course, Republicans will scream bloody murder at the mere mention of "court-packing," accusing Democrats of an unprecedented assault on our democratic institutions and traditions. Given Republican behavior of recent decades, such protests would be risible.

Democrats are rightly proud that we do not threaten to default on the national debt when we do not get our way, or steal Supreme Court vacancies when our party is out of power, or eviscerate the powers of an office after losing control of it (as the Republican-controlled North Carolina legislature did to the state's governorship after the 2016 election). Most Democrats would prefer a world in which both parties played by the established rules. But we cannot continue to fight with one arm tied behind our backs.

*

ABOLISH LIFE TENURE

Eli Noam and Nadine Strossen

Arguably the most important structural problem with the Supreme Court is the justices' lifetime tenure "during good Behavior."

In 1787, when the Constitution was drafted, average life expectancy in the United States was just 36 years. Death itself would limit how long justices served. Today, however, average life expectancy is almost 79 years.

Unsurprisingly, vacancies have become rare. In the past two decades, a vacancy has occurred, on average, once every four years. In the preceding two centuries, vacancies occurred twice as often.

The nine most recent vacancies were created by the death or resignation of justices who had served, on average, 26 years. The average for their 96 predecessors? Just 16 years.

The justices' longer terms on the Court, and the randomness with which the vacancies occur, have several negative consequences.

First, the stakes for presidential appointments have become extraordinarily high, leading to a hyper-intense confirmation process rampant with political and personal attacks.

Second, some presidents have far more appointments than others, and some have none at all. This haphazard distribution of an important presidential power has repercussions that extend for decades beyond the tenure of any given president who appoints a justice. It also incentivizes presidents to select younger, less experienced justices.

Third, justices feel pressure to remain on the Court until an ideologically compatible president again enters the White House. This encourages justices to remain well past their prime. It also reinforces the Court's politicization and reduces the public's respect for it as an institution insulated from partisan influence.

All of these problems could be addressed with a fixed, non-renewable 18-year term for all Supreme Court justices. There would be a vacancy on the Court every two years, and every president would have two appointments during each four-year presidential term.

The regularity of Court vacancies would reduce the stress on the political system. Presidents could appoint distinguished individuals older than 60, and with diverse backgrounds, without fear of forfeiting any influence over the judicial branch.

Eighteen years is hardly a short term of office. It would assure stability, striking the appropriate balance between continuity and change.

If a justice dies or retires during that period, his or her term would be finished by an appointee who would not be eligible for reappointment, thus maintaining the two-year cycle of vacancies.

Some people might fear giving a particular president two or four appointments, and thus reshaping the Court. They might still support the basic principle of a regular fixed tenure, though with a longer term.

This system could be gradually phased in, applied to each future appointment after the adoption of the required constitutional amendment.

Surveys show that the public's trust in the Supreme Court is in decline. It is increasingly seen as just another partisan political institution. Imposing set terms of office would not favor conservatives or liberals. Rather, it would promote the rule of law by reestablishing the Court's credibility as a neutral, principled arbiter.

*

MANDATE DIVERSITY

Sanford Levinson

I have long supported holding a new constitutional convention to address the multiple deficiencies of the Constitution framed in 1787. The organization of the judiciary isn't one of our most pressing constitutional problems, but certain reforms would be highly desirable.

The first piece of business would be to eliminate life tenure for members of the Supreme Court. This could be done through age limits. Almost every state imposes such restrictions on judges in their own courts, as do almost all other national constitutions in the world. But the best solution, already supported by many, would be nonrenewable 18-year terms, which would eliminate the ability of justices to time their resignations for political purposes.

A convention might also raise questions about the appointment process itself. The United States has, without a doubt, the most deeply politicized high court in the world. This was inevitable once the two-party system developed and presidents realized that friendly judges were important to achieving their political goals. At the state level, most judges are elected, a practice that began with the 1846 New York State constitution in an effort to strengthen judicial independence by limiting the power of the governor to appoint his confederates. But there are obvious problems with elected judiciaries, especially in an era of deregulated campaign finance. Instead, many states have moved to forms of "commission" appointment. New Jersey operates under an informal rule that only four of its seven justices can come from a single political party (though Chris Christie tried to violate it). The new Democratic governor, Phil Murphy, recently reappointed one of Christie's unsuccessful nominees when a "Republican seat" became open. Enshrining such a requirement in the Constitution itself could work to defuse tensions at the national level as well.

Finally, we should require a greater diversity of judges. Justice Oliver Wendell Holmes Jr. famously wrote that the life of the law "is not logic" but, rather, "experience." We should be concerned that the current experience of all of the justices is so remarkably narrow. Every single member of the current Court attended either the Harvard or Yale Law Schools (though Justice Ginsburg wound up receiving her degree from Columbia). There is also a distinct East Coast tilt, with three members originally from New York City alone. This is a stunningly large country, with different problems arising in different areas. Anyone who lives in the West is likely to be aware of the vital problems raised by water and its potential scarcity. But of the current justices only Neil Gorsuch and Stephen Breyer were born west of the Mississippi. The Tennessee Constitution requires that its nine justices be chosen equally from the three parts of the state. Wisdom is not concentrated in one region, as a truly representative Supreme Court would reflect.

Incredibly, the present Court is also absent of anyone who has ever run for, let alone held, elective office. Nor is there any justice who ever served on a state court. None since Thurgood Marshall has had the experience of visiting a client in jail, possibly facing a capital murder trial. The Belgian constitution requires that several of its members must have served in the national parliament. There is no reason our Constitution shouldn't be rewritten to include similar stipulations.

*

DOWN WITH JUDICIAL SUPREMACY

Mark Tushnet

What should progressives do about a Supreme Court that's going to be quite conservative for at least 10 or 15 years? Both for strategic reasons and for reasons rooted in political ideals, progressives should start—now—to think seriously about increasing the size of the federal judiciary to offset the packing the Trump administration has already done. A Democratic Congress with a Democratic president can add a lot of judges to the lower federal courts, and they should do so.

If they do, we will hear howls about why "packing the courts" is bad or even unconstitutional, and not simply from conservatives. The "thoughtful" chin-strokers in the nation's major media will join in the criticism. Progressives should be ready to openly defend court-packing as a sensible move in a world where the federal courts have already become highly politicized.

Beyond court-packing, however, progressives should start thinking seriously about the Constitution itself and our tradition of judicial supremacy.

There used to be a progressive tradition of popular constitutionalism. The labor movement around the turn of the 20th century argued passionately that the Constitution guaranteed a right to organize and strike, no matter that the Supreme Court said otherwise. Popular constitutionalism is a practice in which the views of ordinary people about what the Constitution means and does matter more than the views of the Supreme Court. For popular constitutionalists, Supreme Court rulings are interesting data, expressions about the Constitution's meaning that probably ought to be taken seriously but need not be regarded as conclusive.

Some contemporary progressives worry about popular constitutionalism. For them, the point of the Constitution is to protect minorities against oppressive majorities. History suggests that is a utopian vision of the Court, only occasionally matched in practice by its actions. We can be pretty sure that the Supreme Court in the near future isn't going to do much in the way of protecting minorities; the travel-ban decision indicates as much.

The problem of continuing to support judicial supremacy is that the presumably meager minority-protecting benefits of a conservative Court are easily offset by the cost of having a Court that can and will obstruct progressive legislation. At the very least, progressives have to have a serious conversation among themselves about the shibboleth of judicial review and its record of protecting minorities.

Another concern voiced by some progressives about popular constitutionalism is that it means the "yahoos"—ignorant and biased people—will control what the Constitution means. This concern often emerges when progressives suggest it would be a good idea to have another constitutional convention. Many worry about who would control such a convention or that holding it today it would pretty much replicate the politics that have gridlocked Congress.

That might be right—today. But progressives should be thinking and talking about the long term. If progressivism means anything today, it means believing that the good sense of the people of the United States is on our side. All we need to do is bring that good sense to the surface of our daily politics. Popular constitutionalism can help in that task.

We Still Need a Full Court Press

Elie Mystal
November 16, 2020

The rushed confirmation of Justice Amy Coney Barrett has, for the first time in decades, made Democrats think seriously about progressive reforms to the Supreme Court. Today, conservatives hold a 6-3 majority on the court, illegitimately engineered by Donald Trump and Mitch McConnell. This stark reality has radicalized the base. It has even made some Democratic senators consider using their power to achieve deep structural change, as opposed to cosmetic bipartisan redecorating.

Unfortunately, those senators are likely to be in the minority until at least the beginning of 2023. And as long as McConnell remains the majority leader, he is unlikely to allow any reforms (or legislation or democracy) to go forward in the Senate. But Democrats must continue to plan for the day when they have enough seats in the chamber to implement a plan that will mitigate Republican lordship over the Supreme Court.

The easiest solution to the Republican stranglehold is court expansion, or increasing the number of justices. This could be achieved through a simple legislative act and would be inoculated against constitutional challenge because it's been done a bunch of times before. I mean, what would Chief Justice John

Roberts do—lock the doors? The Supreme Court doesn't have an army, so unless he has ninja skills I don't know about, there's little he could do if new colleagues show up for work.

The problem is, court expansion sounds radical to people who don't know how the Constitution works. It sounds political to people who don't realize that increasing the number of justices is the best way to avoid the bare-knuckled partisan fight that happens every time one of the nine justices dies or retires. This has led some Democrats to advance alternative reforms that sound modest but would be, in fact, much more difficult to pull off, because they'd require a reimagining of the Constitution.

The most popular of these ostensibly sober but fundamentally improbable proposals is term limits, which got a substantial boost in September, when Representatives Ro Khanna, Joe Kennedy III, and Don Beyer introduced a bill to restrict the nine justices to single 18-year terms. Their proposal would mean that each president would get to appoint at least two justices to the court per four-year term. The idea is that this would make the court more responsive to electoral politics and end the current practice of letting justices wield power for 30 or 40 years.

Term limits have substantial support, even across party lines. Fix the Court, a group that has been pushing this idea for a while, found that 77 percent of Americans favor some form of term limit. The problem is that they are likely unconstitutional. The Constitution says justices serve "during good behavior," which functionally means they serve for life, absent impeachment. Term limit advocates argue that they could get around this by moving term-limited justices down to the federal courts.

They would still get to serve for life, just not entirely on the Supreme Court.

It's a neat trick, one that I think would be constitutional. Unfortunately, I don't sit on the Supreme Court. The nine people who do are unlikely to agree that they can be kicked off the nation's highest court—particularly the five archconservative justices who claim to be guided strictly by the text of the Constitution and Ouija board messages from James Madison. The proposal would be dead on arrival at the Republican-controlled court that people are trying to reform.

The recognition of this reality has led some Democrats down a more complicated road: jurisdiction stripping. It surprises some people to learn that the Supreme Court's power to declare acts of Congress unconstitutional is not actually in the Constitution. That power, called judicial review, was claimed by the court in the landmark 1803 case *Marbury v. Madison*, and Congress has never stopped it.

One solution to illegitimate Republican control, put forward by Ryan Cooper in *The Week* and Jamelle Bouie in *The New York Times*, among others, would be for a Democratic-controlled Congress to pass legislation stripping courts of the authority to rule on the constitutionality of certain classes of laws. The Constitution spells out limited categories of cases over which the Supreme Court has original jurisdiction, meaning the ones you can take to the Supreme Court without going through the lower courts first. For everything else, the Constitution grants the Supreme Court appellate review, which technically can be limited by Congress.

But there's a hitch: Even if we assume Congress can limit the kinds of cases the Supreme Court reviews, a court that fails to act is just as damaging to rights as one that acts too much. Consider 2018's gerrymandering case *Gill v. Whitford*, in which the court ruled that it did not have the power to strike down gerrymandering that favored Republicans. That decision alone ensures that when we redraw congressional district lines, GOP-controlled state legislatures will be able to gerrymander their candidates into office despite the will of the electorate.

This shouldn't be a surprise. Jurisdiction stripping is a Republican idea. During George W. Bush's administration, the GOP controlled House voted to exempt silly Pledge of Allegiance laws from judicial review. Moreover, vulnerable communities tend to need judicial review, because we can't always anticipate what evil the Republicans will think of next.

What's truly wild, to me, is that jurisdiction stripping is being presented as some kind of moderate alternative to the "radicalism" of court expansion. Ending or limiting judicial review would involve upending the way our system of checks and balances has worked since the earliest days of the country; court expansion would involve changing the number of seats in a body that has been changed multiple times already. Jurisdiction stripping would involve nerfing the power of the Supreme Court because we don't like how it uses its power; court expansion would involve minimizing the importance of any single Supreme Court justice so we don't have to go to the mattresses every time one of them steps down or dies.

Court expansion is constitutional: It has been done before. It is easy: It could be done through simple legislation. It is comprehensive: It could depoliticize the Senate confirmation process and open the door to other changes, like ethics reform. And it is moderate: It wouldn't involve reinventing the system of checks and balances.

But I may have to wait a while to make that argument again. Until the start of 2023 at least, the Supreme Court is secured for Republicans. Then again, the court is poised to make some abhorrent decisions during the next few years—and that almost guarantees that the idea of court expansion will come back around.

If We Don't Reform the Supreme Court, Nothing Else Will Matter

Elie Mystal
February 28, 2020

Not a single significant policy or initiative proposed by the candidates for the Democratic presidential nomination is likely to survive a Supreme Court review. Nothing on guns, nothing on climate, nothing on health care—nothing survives the conservative majority on today's court. Democrats can win the White House with a huge popular mandate, take back the Senate, and nuke the filibuster, but Chief Justice John Roberts and his four associates will still be waiting for them.

If the Democratic candidates are serious about advancing their agenda—be it a progressive agenda or a center-left agenda or a billionaire's agenda—then they have to be serious about undertaking major, structural Supreme Court reform. That reform is not airy wish-casting by a hard left dreaming of revolution. It is the practical first step toward getting any meaningful Democratic policies through all three branches of government. Either court reform happens or nothing happens. People who focus only on Congress or the presidency are like people who plan a road trip thinking only about their eventual destination. They forget that without gas, nobody is going anywhere.

Court reform can take a variety of forms, some blunt and partisan, others intricate and geared toward balance. But at its core,
Supreme Court reform involves shaking up the configuration of
the court. And at its core, it is constitutional. That's because the
Constitution provides Congress with wide latitude in structur-
ing the court.

The Supreme Court (and all federal courts) are established by
Article III of the Constitution. And Article III has only this to
say about the structure of the Supreme Court:

> The judicial Power of the United States, shall be vested in one
> supreme Court, and in such inferior Courts as the Congress
> may from time to time ordain and establish. The Judges, both
> of the supreme and inferior Courts, shall hold their Offices
> during good Behaviour, and shall, at stated Times, receive
> for their Services, a Compensation, which shall not be dimin-
> ished during their Continuance in Office.

That is founding-father-speak for "Whatever. We'll figure this
part out later."

In fact, it took the country a long time to figure out how to
structure the Supreme Court. The first version of the court had
six justices. John Adams and his congressional allies changed
that number to five in the months after his loss to Thomas
Jefferson to prevent him from filling a judicial seat. Jefferson
quickly repealed that law, putting the number back to six, and
later added a seventh justice, because why not? Andrew Jackson
pushed the court to nine justices; Congress added a 10th during the Civil War and then pulled it back to seven in 1866 as

payback to President Andrew Johnson for, among other things, vetoing the Reconstruction Acts. Then everybody got over themselves. The current number of nine justices has been set since the Judiciary Act of 1869.

Only one serious effort to change the number of justices has been made since then, and most people have heard about it. Frustrated by a court that stood against his New Deal programs, Franklin Roosevelt proposed the Judicial Procedures Reform Bill of 1937. It would have allowed him to appoint up to six new justices to the court, for a total of 15. Democrats and Republicans alike opposed the bill, and it failed miserably. Between the unpopular proposal and an economic downturn, the Democrats hemorrhaged seats in the midterm elections of 1938. In the ensuing decades, nobody seriously attempted to futz with the Supreme Court again.

Until Mitch McConnell came along.

After Justice Antonin Scalia died in February of 2016, majority leader McConnell and the Senate Republicans unilaterally decided to change the number of Supreme Court justices from nine to eight for the remainder of President Barack Obama's term. It was a scheme every bit as cynical and partisan as what Adams had tried to do to Jefferson, only McConnell's gambit worked.

One year later, with the help of President Donald Trump, McConnell was able to replace Scalia with Neil Gorsuch. Then, to spike the football, Trump and McConnell responded to the retirement of Justice Anthony Kennedy (a swing voter on the court) by installing a hard-core conservative who was accused of attempted rape, Brett Kavanaugh. We're now looking at a Supreme Court staffed for a generation with an illegitimate justice and a morally repugnant one.

Because of McConnell's brazen maneuvers, court reform is suddenly back in vogue. Many of the Democratic presidential candidates have indicated an openness to the idea, while scholars and think tanks are pumping out reform proposals. Some of these favor reform in its rawest, tit-for-tat form: packing the court with two new justices to make up for what McConnell pulled with Gorsuch and Kavanaugh. But the idea of court reform is much broader, more nuanced, and frankly less partisan than what both proponents and detractors of court packing may imagine. There are proposals focused on changing how we choose Supreme Court justices. There are proposals centered on limiting the lifetime power of justices. There are proposals that seek to make the Supreme Court work more like every other federal court. And there are proposals addressing judicial ethics and the simple and noble goal of keeping people who have been credibly accused of sexual misconduct off the highest court in the land.

Some or all of these proposals can work. While reforming the Supreme Court is a legal issue—a number of the plans raise real constitutional questions—it is also, perhaps even primarily, a political issue. As Sean McElwee, the director of research and polling for the reform group Take Back the Court, told *Politico*, "We have too long tried to take on the court with the tools of law, but if the court is in fact a political branch, then instead of using the tools of law, you need to use the tools of politics."

The public can be motivated on this issue, but it needs to understand that the fight is not for a Democratic Party Court but a functional one. Court reform is not a revenge fantasy; it is an attempt to restore the Supreme Court to legitimacy and fairness.

There are now three main ideas for reforming the court: adding moderates to its bench, imposing de facto term limits, and enlarging it with more ideologically diverse justices who are bound to ethical guidelines.

Let's define what those ideas actually mean and stop allowing Republicans to define them for us.

Mandated Moderation

Among the Democrats running for president, former South Bend mayor Pete Buttigieg has stood out as the only contender who has embraced a specific court reform plan. Other candidates, like Senators Bernie Sanders and Elizabeth Warren, have indicated that they are open to the idea. Some candidates, like former vice president Joe Biden, simply promise to nominate better judges. But Buttigieg has made court reform a signature part of his campaign.

His court reform plan, colloquially dubbed 5-5-5, is largely cribbed from a *Yale Law Journal* feature, "How to Save the Supreme Court," by law professors Daniel Epps and Ganesh Sitaraman (who is a senior adviser to Warren). The core of the proposal is to expand the Supreme Court to 15 justices: five conservatives, five liberals, and five moderates, with each of the last group chosen by a vote of the 10 partisan justices. The 10 partisans would have traditional lifetime tenure. But the moderates, called visiting justices, would serve one-year terms, would be selected two years in advance, and would be chosen from the existing crop of Circuit Court of Appeals or District Court judges. Should the 10 partisan justices fail to agree on a moderate slate, the Supreme Court would lack a quorum and be unable to hear cases that year. As Epps and Sitaraman explain, a key point of this plan is to decrease the partisanship and rancor that now surrounds the Supreme Court:

Finally, the visiting Justices—and the explicit partisan-balance requirements—would significantly reduce the stakes of Supreme Court nominations. Because each political party would hold a set number of seats, and because additional Justices would join the Court no matter what, the fate of issues like abortion would never turn on any one confirmation battle.

Buttigieg understands this challenge implicitly. As he has remarked on the campaign trail, his very right to be married came down to the vote of one Supreme Court justice. In defense of the 5-5-5 plan, he told *Vox*, "We need to make serious reforms to the Supreme Court to restore American's trust in the institution and make it less political."

The 5-5-5 theory is wonderful, but it might not survive contact with reality. The first challenge is that the idea of a moderate judge is largely a myth. A judge who is seemingly moderate in one area of the law might be a whacked-out extremophile in some other area.

Consider former justice Kennedy. On the campaign trail, Buttigieg has held him up as an example of someone who would fit the definition of a moderate under the 5-5-5 plan. Kennedy gets this mantle because he sometimes broke with Republican orthodoxy, at least in the areas of LGBTQ equality and abortion rights.

But Kennedy, a Ronald Reagan appointee, was also a First Amendment absolutist whose extreme positions led him to write the *Citizens United* decision, which more or less destroyed campaign finance reform in this country. He might not have been the most fire-breathing conservative justice, but he was certainly a justice who sided time and again with cases that supported the Republican or Trumpian agenda. It was Kennedy who provided conservatives with the fifth vote they needed to ruin gun regulations in *District of Columbia v. Heller*, and he was the fifth vote in *Trump v. Hawaii*, the case addressing Trump's Muslim ban.

The legacy of a justice like Kennedy highlights the challenge of finding moderates at any level of the judiciary. But there's a second, perhaps more serious problem with the plan. The Constitution quite clearly gives the president the power to appoint justices; it says nothing about the members of the Supreme Court getting to choose their own colleagues.

Here is the appointments clause as it appears in Article II of the Constitution:

> [The president] shall nominate, and by and with the Advice and Consent of the Senate, shall appoint Ambassadors, other public Ministers and Consuls, Judges of the supreme Court, and all other Officers of the United States, whose Appointments are not herein otherwise provided for, and

which shall be established by Law: but the Congress may by
Law vest the Appointment of such inferior Officers, as they
think proper, in the President alone, in the Courts of Law, or
in the Heads of Departments.

That seems fairly straightforward. It says the president "shall nominate" and the Senate can "consent" to the appointments of ambas-
sadors, public ministers, and "judges of the Supreme Court." Epps
and Sitaraman try to get around this by arguing that the visiting
justices would be "inferior officers," and thus their appointments
could be delegated by Congress to the Supreme Court.

Perhaps. But here's the thing to remember when debating the
constitutionality of any court reform plan: It's the current
Supreme Court, stacked as it is with conservative appointments,
that will make the final decision as to whether a plan is constitutional. Who wants to be the one to tell Roberts that his power
should be greatly reduced because his institution is full of partisan hacks and is broken beyond repair?

Buttigieg says that 5-5-5 is just one idea he's floating and that
he's open to other solutions. This particular reform plan is what
a fair-minded Supreme Court would reasonably look like. But we
might need better justices, working with politicians who are better
humans, operating under a better Constitution, to actually get there.

Forever Is a Long Time

A central goal of 5-5-5 and similar reform plans is to address
the partisanship and politicization of the Supreme Court.
But there are other proposals that accept the fundamentally

political nature of the court and simply try to manage the issue in a fairer, less rancorous way. Term limits would be one way to achieve this, largely by making sure that the randomness of death (and the luck of the party that happens to be in power at the time) does not have generational consequences on our rights and freedoms.

The problem with term limits is our antiquated Constitution. Article III is pretty clear that Supreme Court justices hold their appointments for life: "The Judges, both of the supreme and inferior Courts, shall hold their Offices during good Behaviour." You can tell this line was written at a time when nobody got flu shots and people could die from pissing off Aaron Burr.

Yet there is a solution to the constitutional mandate of lifetime appointments, and it has already been implemented in every "inferior Court" in the country. Lower federal courts are still subject to Article III, but they offer judges the opportunity to take "senior status."

Senior status is established by statute and has been deemed perfectly constitutional. It's a semiretirement option offered to judges who reach 65 years of age and have achieved the Rule of 80—that is, their age plus their number of years in service on the federal bench equals 80. Senior judges still take cases, at their discretion or the discretion of the chief judge of their circuit. They still draw a full salary. In fact, over 30 percent of federal Circuit Court judges (just one step below the Supreme Court) have senior status, and those judges handle about 15 percent of circuit cases. But they don't formally take up seats, which means that a president can nominate others to replace them.

When the full circuit sits to review a case, only active judges typically participate.

The Supreme Court doesn't do this, but it could. Fix the Court, a group dedicated to reforming the Supreme Court, has perhaps the clearest term-limit proposal. New justices would be limited to a single 18-year term. Those terms would be staggered so that no one president would get to name a disproportionate number of justices. When their terms are over, the justices would take senior status at full salary, avoiding the problem of lifetime tenure.

The idea of staggering justices across presidential terms is key. The obvious partisanship around Supreme Court retirements is one of the worst features of our current system. Kennedy, for instance, retired specifically so that a Republican president could appoint his replacement. He's healthy, and if Hillary Clinton had won the Electoral College in 2016, he'd likely still be on the bench. Yet we find ourselves in a situation where 86-year-old Ruth Bader Ginsburg has to live until at least January 20, 2021, or women's rights will be lost. Staggered term limits would ensure that electoral winners shaped the Supreme Court, not the Grim Reaper.

In recent years, the logic of this approach has become more popular. Polls have shown that a majority of Democrats and Republicans support term limits for justices. Fix the Court's plan was recently endorsed in an open letter signed by 63 legal scholars from across the ideological spectrum. Conservative columnist John Fund has written positively about the proposal in *National Review*, of all places. Former presidential candidate Andrew Yang is on record as supporting the plan. Bernie

Sanders has expressed interest in some version of term limits. Even one current Supreme Court justice, Stephen Breyer, has applauded the idea. "I think it would be fine to have long terms, say 18 years or something like that, for a Supreme Court justice," he said. "It would make life easier. You know, I wouldn't have to worry about when I'm going to retire or not."

But there's a catch. Just because senior status has been deemed a constitutional option for the lower courts doesn't mean the same can hold true for the Supreme Court. As Harvard Law professor Laurence Tribe, a proponent of term limits in theory, explained the difficulties to me, "For several years, I was inclined to favor term limits, but I'm increasingly doubtful that the Supreme Court, as currently composed, would agree that Article III can be interpreted the way it would have to be in order to make Supreme Court appointments terminable after a fixed number of years. ... That, in turn, suggests that the massive effort and political capital that would be required to get a federal statute enacted limiting the terms of Supreme Court justices just wouldn't be worth it."

This is the most difficult barrier for many court reform proposals: the current Supreme Court. While Congress can add justices without the need for constitutional review, the most innovative and nonpartisan reforms require the partisan Supreme Court to agree.

For Tribe, this leads us back to where we more or less started. "That leaves only old-fashioned court packing, which I'm open to discussing but have serious political—though not constitutional—doubts about," he said.

Supreme Circuit

The most inelegant and politically charged version of court reform is, ironically, the version least likely to be quashed by the Republicans on the Supreme Court. We know that raw, unadulterated court packing is constitutional because changing the number of justices has been done multiple times in our history. With enough political power in the Senate and the White House, Democrats could add two, four, even 100 justices and simply dare Republicans to pull off the same feat the next time they're in control.

This kind of tit-for-tat might be a satisfying response to McConnell's manipulation of the court. And it solves, or at least salves, the problem of Gorsuch's illegitimacy and Kavanaugh's alleged immorality. But adding, say, two justices is not really a reform. It's revenge.

There is, however, a way to reimagine court packing as a form of judicial reform instead of partisan reprisal. The reform involves making the Supreme Court operate like the Circuit Courts of Appeal. These courts are partisan, to be sure, but they're not facing the same legitimacy crisis that we're seeing on the Supreme Court. That's because, in addition to the fact that many have more members, they have two things the Supreme Court doesn't have: panels and ethics.

Once they're appealed to the circuit court, most cases are initially heard by a three-judge panel. These panels are chosen at random from the members of that circuit. The panel renders a decision, and most of the time, that ruling is final. It takes a vote by a majority of the circuit to agree to have the case heard en banc (that is, in front of a full court). Only a vanishingly small percentage of cases ever make it there. The Second Circuit, for instance, hears less than 1 percent of its cases en banc.

Panels are great for the appearance of legitimacy. The random wheel makes it impossible to predict which judges will get which case and thus the way that a case will go. The court can still overrule a panel en banc, but again, it takes a majority to do so. That's a significant contrast with the way the current Supreme Court operates. It takes only four votes—a minority—for the court to grant certiorari and agree to hear a case as a full body.

Panels don't remove partisanship from the lower courts. There's a reason Democratic state attorneys general rush to the Ninth Circuit and the Republicans rush to the Fifth. But that's why adding justices is a critical part of reform. Packing the court could mean more diversity—more ethnic diversity, more gender diversity, more diversity of thought and experience. That diversity itself would be a moderating influence on the court.

While I said earlier in this piece that moderate justices don't really exist, moderate opinions are written all the time. They come into being when judges write opinions as narrowly as possible in order to attract a majority of their colleagues to sign on to them. The Ninth Circuit operates with 29 active judges, the Fifth Circuit with up to 17. In the case of en banc hearings, it's almost impossible to imagine a string of 15-14 or 9-8 cases on those circuits that would have the same sweeping impact as the torrent of 5-4 opinions we can expect from the Supreme Court this June.

Moving the Supreme Court to a panel system is an idea that reformers, scholars, and even some judges have suggested. But to finish the job of making the Supreme Court act like a real court and less like the enforcement arm for whichever party holds a majority, we need to add one final condition: ethics reform.

The Supreme Court is the only court in the land whose judges operate under no ethical guidelines. The Constitution says the justices hold their positions while in "good Behaviour," yet nobody has defined precisely what that entails for these nine people. I'd argue that sexual harassment is not good behavior. I'd argue that attempted rape and lying under oath are not good behavior. I'd also argue that holding a meeting and taking a picture with people who have active business before the court is textbook unethical and, as on any other court, should require justices to recuse themselves from that active matter.

Yet we live in a world in which Kavanaugh and Justice Samuel Alito can and do meet with a member of the National Organization for Marriage, an anti-LGBTQ group that has filed an amicus brief in a case that the court is considering on whether gay and transgender workers are protected under the Civil Rights Act. We live in a world in which Justice Clarence Thomas regularly hocks himself out to partisan Federalist Society events. Nobody can stop them from doing this, because the ethical rules that govern a random traffic court judge in Peoria do not apply to the Supreme Court justices.

Simply subjecting the justices to the same ethical rules that govern all other lifetime-appointed federal judges would be a sea change in terms of how the court operates. The partisan bias that is now so open that it threatens public faith in the court would at least have to be tamped down. Even more important, ethics reform would open the door to the kind of accountability that's been needed since long before the Me Too era. A lifetime appointment cannot be a license for past or present sexual harassment.

Roberts has long resisted ethics reform (though he has recently been alleged to be studying the issue). That's how I arrive at my preferred number for court packing: 10 additional justices, to overrule the nine others who may consider themselves beyond ethical accountability. A 19-member Supreme Court, hearing most cases in panels and subject to ethical standards, would look, feel, and act more like every other federal court. It would still be a partisan institution, and it could still be manipulated via deaths and retirements, but uplifting the Supreme Court to the standards in place for the lower courts would still count as meaningful reform.

There's one final advantage to coupling court packing with ethics reform. If the Democrats win the White House and take back the Senate, adding 10 justices would give them the political leverage to make the Republicans an offer they couldn't refuse: If they agreed to bipartisan support of a judicial reform package, then the 10 new justices could be evenly split between Democratic and Republican nominees—allowing Republicans to maintain their current, ill-gotten, one-vote majority. Reducing Kavanaugh to one of 19 and subjecting him to ethical strictures are bigger long-term goals than expanding the court to 11 and hoping Republicans never win the presidency again.

History has shown us that purely partisan court packing doesn't work or is easily overcome by the next administration. Nonetheless, court packing might be the only tool for court reform the Constitution currently allows. Most reformers want a scalpel, but the Constitution has perhaps provided only a hammer. Still, in the right hands, a hammer can be used to build something.

*

Supreme Court reform remains a nascent preoccupation, limited largely to wonks and advocates, but some kind of reform must happen under the next Democratic administration, whenever that is. Republicans have changed the rules when it comes to Supreme Court appointments. We can't just go back to the way things were before Kavanaugh, before Gorsuch, and before McConnell.

The Republicans didn't win the Supreme Court in one day or in one election. They spent a generation figuring out how to take control of it. They poured money and political resources into promoting their vision, and they built an entire infrastructure to help them pull off a full-scale heist of the Supreme Court in broad daylight.

Democrats must battle back. These court reform proposals are the first wave. They're good. They're nonpartisan. If Democrats can't win cases at the Supreme Court, winning anywhere else won't really matter.

The Long, Troubled History of the Supreme Court—and How We Can Change It

Louis Michael Seidman
June 20, 2022

By now, it should be abundantly clear that our antiquated Constitution, written over two centuries ago by white men to govern a small, slave-dependent republic huddled along the Eastern Seaboard, does not meet the needs of the sprawling, multiethnic, and complicated country that we have become.

For anyone who doubts this proposition, consider the following facts. In two out of the last six presidential elections, a candidate became president even though he lost the popular vote. Virtually all of the money and attention in presidential elections are devoted to a tiny number of swing states that determine the outcome. The Constitution vests in state legislatures the power to appoint presidential electors whether or not they are chosen by a popular majority—a power that Donald Trump tried to take advantage of in 2020, and may well take advantage of in 2024.

Additionally, nine individuals, appointed for life and responsible to no one, regularly make crucial and unreviewable decisions about matters such as the structure of health care in the

United States, the nature of marriage, the right of women to reproductive justice, and the powers of the federal government and the states. All the justices on the Supreme Court insist that they are neutral and apolitical public servants who do no more than follow "the law" as it is written. Yet they are nominated by a process drenched in raw partisanship, and their votes regularly align with the partisan views of the people who appoint them. Republican presidents have appointed 15 of the last 22 justices to the Supreme Court, even though they won the popular vote in only five of the last 15 elections. The last Democrat to serve as chief justice was Fred Vinson, whose brief and largely undistinguished career ended almost 70 years ago.

The Constitution protects the rights of people who want to make movies catering to individuals who get sexual pleasure from witnessing the sadistic crushing of innocent animals. Yet it doesn't explicitly protect the rights of women, and it does nothing to protect the rights of all of us to live in a world that is not ravaged by global warming.

Huge popular majorities favor measures including more effective gun regulation, limitations on campaign spending, and reductions to the cost of prescription drugs, yet because of the political structures that the framers imposed on us, we are unable to accomplish those objectives.

These facts, and many more like them, should make any sensible person skeptical about our Constitution and about the role it plays in modern political culture. And yet constitutional skeptics almost never get a fair hearing. Instead, American politics is saturated by reverence for an ancient and anachronistic document, written by people who in many cases owned other human beings, and never endorsed by a majority of the inhabitants of our country.

Liberals and conservatives, Democrats and Republicans, Congress members and Supreme Court justices, all insist on their own partisan versions of constitutional obedience while our political culture collapses, crucial public needs go unmet, and the ties that bind us together as a country fray. We need to understand that conventional constitutionalism is irrational and wrong. It attaches religious significance to a decidedly secular and deeply flawed document. It is standing in the way of saving our country. It has got to stop.

*

Perhaps the most inviting target for constitutional skepticism is the United States Supreme Court. There is no necessary association between the Supreme Court and American constitutionalism. All federal officeholders take an oath to support and defend the Constitution, and one could imagine a system in which the Constitution was enforced by Congress, the president, and state officials. Still, in American constitutional culture, the Supreme Court has assumed such a central role that it is often taken to be the embodiment of constitutionalism.

The justices themselves do everything they can to promote this image. They protect their reputation by working in secret. According to hallowed tradition, no one other than the justices attends the sessions where cases are actually decided. The justices rarely hold press conferences or make public statements.

Moreover, the quasi-religious claptrap that surrounds the court—the robes the justices wear, the marble temple in which they are housed, the solemnity and formality of the oral arguments that they conduct—is meant to symbolize the grandeur, neutrality, impersonality, and majesty of the law, and of the Constitution whence it derives.

An interlocking web of myths buttresses this imagery. The justices are thought to be brilliant jurists who work extraordinarily hard. They are wise women and men who take the long view and are above the petty squabbling that engulfs the rest of the government. They are apolitical public servants who lead monastic existences devoted solely to the rule of law. Their independence guarantees that they are answerable to no political party or faction, but solely to their conscience and to the US Constitution.

All of this is arrant nonsense. Historically, the Supreme Court of the United States has been populated mostly by people of decidedly ordinary intellect and ability who have gotten pretty cushy jobs through their political connections. The notion that independence—insulation from political accountability—guarantees that justices will be motivated by devotion to the law rests on a logical fallacy and has little empirical support. In fact, unaccountability produces just what one would expect: a freedom to indulge personal quirks and obsessions.

Here are just a few examples of the judicial failings that should give any thoughtful court observer pause:

§ In the early 19th century, John Marshall saw no problem with serving as secretary of state and chief justice of the United States at the same time. In perhaps the most famous case in American legal history, *Marbury v. Madison*, Marshall as chief justice ruled on the legal implications of actions taken by Marshall as secretary of state.

§ Also during the 19th century, Justice Henry Baldwin was hospitalized for "incurable lunacy" and missed an entire term of the court. He nonetheless returned to the bench and remained on the court for years. Richard Peters Jr., the Supreme Court's reporter of decisions, stated that "most courtroom observers of Baldwin agreed that *'his mind is out of order.'*"

§ Justice Robert Grier, who had suffered a disabling stroke, cast the deciding vote in one of the most crucial decisions in American history, holding that Congress lacked the power to make paper money legal tender. Unfortunately, it appears that he acted without having any clear idea of what case he was voting on.

§ Justice James McReynolds was a notorious racist and anti-Semite. He was unremittingly hostile to his colleague Louis Brandeis because Brandeis was a Jew. When Charles Hamilton Houston, the renowned African American civil rights attorney, argued before the court in 1938, McReynolds turned his back on him. He also referred to Howard University as the "[n———] university."

§ Justice Charles Whittaker was often unable to decide how to vote or to keep up with his work. Once, when assigned to write a majority opinion, he ended up turning the task over to Justice William O. Douglas, who, out of pity, ghostwrote it for him even though Douglas had also written the dissenting opinion.

§ Shortly after he was confirmed as a justice, Hugo Black faced a huge scandal about his membership in the Ku Klux Klan. Reporters for the *Pittsburgh Post-Gazette* discovered that although he had officially resigned from the Klan at the beginning of his campaign for the US Senate, Black rejoined the organization and was given a lifetime membership.

§ After becoming an associate justice, Abe Fortas regularly provided advice to his former client, President Lyndon Johnson, even though the Johnson administration was often a party before the court. Fortas was forced to resign when it became known that he had accepted payments from various interests with potential business before the court.

§ While serving as a law clerk for Justice Robert Jackson, William Rehnquist prepared a memorandum arguing that the court should reaffirm the "separate but equal" doctrine announced in *Plessy v. Ferguson*. When confronted with the memo at his confirmation hearing, Rehnquist swore under oath that, contrary to what the memo in fact said and despite persuasive evidence from contemporaries, it did not reflect his personal views.

§ During oral argument in an employment discrimination case, Chief Justice Warren Burger announced that women were better at secretarial work than men were. He reportedly told his law clerks that Blacks made talented gardeners because they had a great sense of color, but that they could not get mortgages the way Jews did because Jews were generally more able and trustworthy. Women should not be allowed to serve as judges in rape trials, he added, because they were too emotional and incapable of fair judgment.

There are enough examples of this sort of behavior to be troubling. (And this is without touching on the misconduct of modern justices—for example, Brett Kavanaugh's bizarre and likely perjurous testimony before the Senate Judiciary Committee, or Clarence Thomas's blatantly partisan extrajudicial diatribes.) Moreover, the secrecy that surrounds the court means that we have no way to know how many other instances of incompetence, misconduct, or florid eccentricity have influenced the court's work. Still, I do not mean to claim that these examples are representative. No doubt most justices have done their best at what is a difficult job.

In some ways, the more serious problem is not flagrant incompetence or mendacity but plain-vanilla mediocrity. For every Louis Brandeis, there are many Sherman Mintons. For every William Brennan, there are many Gabriel Duvalls. The truth is that most of the justices have gained their seats because of inside connections, political deals, or ideological commitments. Their performance on the bench is consistent with what one would expect from individuals selected on this basis.

If one looks at paper credentials, the modern court scores higher than the historical average. All of today's justices have distinguished academic records, and there is no reason to doubt their intelligence. That said, their range of experience is limited. None of the justices has had to meet a payroll for a private business or make decisions outside of a huge bureaucracy. None has run for or served in elective office. Although the Supreme Court hears many criminal cases every year, no sitting justice has ever served as a criminal defense attorney, although this will change when

Ketanji Brown Jackson joins. The court regularly decides technical and complex cases about specialized matters like patent law and employee benefits law, but no sitting justice has devoted significant time to studying these matters. The court's opinions routinely rely on empirical assumptions, but the justices appear woefully ignorant of statistical method. There is little evidence that many of them know much about the social sciences, much less about philosophy, literature, or the hard sciences.

Perhaps more significantly, no one should confuse the justices with apolitical and neutral students of jurisprudence. Many of them got their jobs because they were connected to politically powerful figures. Consider in this respect Justice Antonin Scalia's unintentionally damning defense of his failure to recuse himself from a case in which Vice President Dick Cheney was a named party after Scalia had gone duck hunting with him:

Many Justices have reached this Court precisely because they were friends of the incumbent President or other senior officials—and from the earliest days down to modern times Justices have had close personal relationships with the President and other officers of the Executive. John Quincy Adams hosted dinner parties featuring such luminaries as Chief Justice Marshall, Justices Johnson, Story, and Todd. ... Justice Harlan and his wife often "stopped in" at the White House to see the Hayes family and pass a Sunday evening in a small group, visiting and singing hymns. Justice Stone tossed around a medicine ball with members of the Hoover administration mornings outside the White House. Justice Douglas was a regular at President

Franklin Roosevelt's poker parties; Chief Justice Vinson played poker with President Truman.

Modern justices have also been cozy with political figures, and their prior service has established deep ties of personal and political loyalty. Here are some examples:

§ In his younger years, Chief Justice John Roberts served as associate White House counsel for Ronald Reagan and as the principal deputy in the Solicitor General's Office for George H.W. Bush.

§ Justice Samuel Alito worked as assistant solicitor general and at the Office of Legal Counsel under Reagan.

§ Justice Stephen Breyer worked in the Johnson Justice Department and was special counsel to the Senate Judiciary Committee while it was under Democratic control.

§ Justice Elena Kagan befriended Barack Obama while they were both teaching at the University of Chicago Law School. She went on to serve as special counsel to the Senate Judiciary Committee under Joe Biden, as associate White House counsel and deputy assistant to the president for domestic policy under Bill Clinton, and as solicitor general under Obama.

§ Justice Kavanaugh drafted the Starr Report, which claimed that Clinton had committed potentially impeachable offenses; worked for the George W. Bush campaign on the Florida recount in 2000; and served as Bush's staff secretary in the White House.

There is nothing dishonorable about service in any of these positions. Still, it strains credulity to believe that the justices suddenly shed their political predispositions upon assuming the bench.

*

None of this would matter much but for the fact that the justices exercise extraordinary power—and throughout the court's history, they have used this power to render many, many truly terrible decisions. This is not the place for a comprehensive history of the Supreme Court, but some highlights from that history convey a sense of the role that the court has played in our political and legal culture.

In the earliest days of the republic, Federalist judges, including Supreme Court justices, vigorously enforced the Alien and Sedition Acts, which criminalized criticism of the president and resulted in the jailing of opposition leaders throughout the country.

In the run-up to the Civil War, the court consistently sided with slave owners. For example, in *Prigg v. Pennsylvania*, Justice Joseph Story, writing for the court, held that a Pennsylvania law that prohibited the extradition of African Americans for the purpose of enslaving them was unconstitutional. In the *Dred Scott* decision, Chief Justice Roger Taney, writing for the court, held that even free African Americans could not be citizens of the United States and that Congress's efforts to outlaw slavery in the territories were unconstitutional.

After the Civil War, Congress enacted Reconstruction legislation that amounted to a comprehensive program to eradicate the "badges and incidents of slavery" and to protect the newly freed men and women from violence and discrimination. Fearful of judicial interference, the Reconstruction Congress enacted the 14th Amendment to insulate its program from constitutional attack. Unfortunately, the court read the amendment in an indefensibly narrow fashion and proceeded to invalidate much of the Reconstruction program.

When political pressure on the South eased, Southern states enacted a comprehensive system of racial apartheid. In *Plessy v. Ferguson*, the court, in an infamous opinion by Justice Henry Billings Brown, found that this "separate but equal" regime was constitutionally permissible.

The court did no better at enforcing civil liberties during this period. Throughout the 19th century, it regularly ignored infringements on speech and free exercise rights. In an especially shameful decision, the court gave its approval to a massive eugenics program that resulted in the forced sterilization of thousands of women.

With American entry into World War I, the Wilson administration embarked on a vigorous program to suppress dissent, utilizing the Espionage Act of 1917 and Sedition Act of 1918 to jail many opponents of the war. The court upheld these convictions in every case that came before it, including the conviction of the Socialist Party leader Eugene Debs, who received millions of votes for president while sitting in a jail cell.

In the late 19th and early 20th centuries, populism and progressivism emerged as an important political force, and state governments began to enact various forms of economic regulation.

For example, state statutes mandated minimum wages and maximum hours; prohibited "yellow dog contracts," which prevented workers from forming unions; and provided for the price regulation of public utilities. The Supreme Court's response to these reforms was uncertain and inconsistent but, in general, hostile.

In 1905, for instance, the Supreme Court decided *Lochner v. New York*. According to the court, a state statute protecting employees of bakery shops from having to work more than 10 hours per day and 60 hours per week violated the "freedom of contract" protected by the 14th Amendment's due process clause. And *Lochner* was hardly an outlier. In all, between 1905 and 1930, the court invalidated some 200 statutes imposing economic regulation.

Concern about the court's ideological motivations came to a head during the New Deal period, when the court blocked some important New Deal programs and threatened to invalidate many more. After his overwhelming victory in 1936, President Franklin Roosevelt moved to discipline the court by increasing its size from nine to 15 justices. Congress ultimately rejected the proposal, but the court more or less backed off from confrontation with a popular president. Roosevelt remained in office long enough to appoint eight justices, and these appointments inaugurated a period during which the court abstained from interfering with economic regulation.

At the same time, the Roosevelt Court's defense of civil liberties was, at best, spotty. The court occasionally defended the rights of unpopular speakers, but in moments when civil liberties were at greatest risk, it refused to intervene. After the Japanese attack on Pearl Harbor, the Roosevelt administration ordered the exclusion of thousands of Japanese American citizens from their homes. The Supreme Court held that the action was constitutionally permissible, even though the exclusion was based solely on ethnicity and the excluded individuals were given no opportunity to demonstrate their loyalty.

When the McCarthy panic hit the country in the postwar period, the liberal justices again caved to public pressure. They acceded to the criminal convictions and firings of scores of people because of their political affiliations.

*

Due to a series of historical accidents, by the late 1950s power on the court had shifted to justices who viewed themselves as legal reformers. During the brief heyday of the Warren Court, the justices acted vigorously to dismantle racial apartheid in the South, reform the criminal justice system, protect the free speech rights of dissenters, require equality of population in voting districts, and provide some constitutional protection for poverty-stricken Americans. Even after Chief Justice Earl Warren had retired and a conservative president had somewhat changed the complexion of the court, it rendered pathbreaking decisions protecting reproductive autonomy and attacking gender discrimination.

A half-century later, the Warren Court's hold on the American imagination remains strong. For many conservatives, the Warren Court remains an exemplar of arrogant and lawless judicial overreach. Its more important impact, though, has been on the attitude of many progressives. Anyone looking at the entire sweep of the court's history would understand that the court has pretty consistently stood with the most shortsighted and venal impulses in American society. Still, the Warren Court interregnum supports the hope that if only the right justices could somehow be appointed, the Supreme Court might yet be an engine driving us toward the Preamble's promise that we "establish justice." That hope, in turn, softens the criticism that many progressives might otherwise direct toward the court.

In evaluating this hope, it is important to emphasize two points about the Warren Court. First, this judicial Camelot did not last very long—effectively only 10 years. Second, for all its ambition, the Warren Court's actual accomplishments were limited and fragile. Dismantling the Jim Crow system was an important achievement, but as many scholars have pointed out, the court's orders were widely ignored. Real change did not come until Lyndon Johnson's huge victory in the 1964 election and the breaking of the Southern stranglehold on Congress.

Many other Warren Court reforms were similarly vexed. The court addressed some of the worst manifestations of police violence and lawlessness, but it also invented the concept of "qualified immunity" for government officials who violated civil rights, thereby shielding them from meaningful legal accountability. It was Chief Justice Warren himself who wrote for the court in *Terry v. Ohio* to endorse the "stop and frisk" tactics that resulted in the systematic harassment of millions of Black men.

*

The Supreme Court's history is important and often misunderstood, but the crucial question to answer is how the court operates now and how it is likely to operate in the immediate future. Unfortunately, whatever our experience during the Warren Court era, the modern Supreme Court has returned to its historical role as the defender of class privilege, racial hierarchy, and misogyny. From the invalidation of campaign finance legislation, to the hobbling of efforts to control climate change, to the recent threat to abortion rights, the justices have allied themselves with the most reactionary forces in American life.

So what is to be done? In the wake of the Senate's unprecedented refusal to consider President Obama's nomination of Merrick Garland to the court and the debacle surrounding the nomination of Brett Kavanaugh, academics and political figures have proposed a variety of reforms. The simplest to implement would be an expansion of the court's size. The Constitution does not require that there be only nine justices, and the court's size has varied throughout our history. A variant of this proposal would allow the court's size to fluctuate so as to allow each administration a set number of appointments.

Other, more complex proposals would change the court's functioning in dramatic ways. For example, the political analyst Norman Ornstein has proposed 18-year term limits for Supreme Court justices, with a justice then relegated to service on the lower courts so as not to run afoul of the constitutional guarantee of life tenure. Former presidential candidate Pete Buttigieg has borrowed from a far-reaching proposal advanced by law professors Daniel Epps and Ganesh Sitaraman. Under this scheme, there would be 15 justices, with 10 equally divided between the two parties and those 10 choosing the remaining five.

Here are some other proposals that the Supreme Court itself could adopt in the unlikely event that it were so inclined:

§ *Ditch the robes and the "Your Honors."* Supreme Court justices are not gods or priests; they are ordinary human beings. In a country without an aristocracy, respect should never be based on station. Instead, it must be earned and is always held provisionally. The justices should act, and should be treated, like every other citizen.

§ *Require a seven-justice majority to invalidate a statute.* Nothing in the Constitution mandates majority voting by the justices; indeed, by internal rule, the court has deviated from majority voting in deciding whether to grant review over cases. More than 100 years ago, the famed Harvard Law School professor James Bradley Thayer wrote that a statute should be invalidated only when its unconstitutionality was "so clear that it is not open to rational question." A way to institutionalize Thayer's insight is to require at least a seven-justice majority to invalidate a statute. If three justices think that the statute is constitutional, it is hard to say that their judgment is "irrational." Why, then, should the judgment of six justices prevail over the collective judgment of three of their colleagues and the political branches?

§ *Media coverage.* For years, there has been argument about whether the Supreme Court's oral arguments should be broadcast live on television. The court seems to be moving haltingly in this direction, but this change does not go nearly far enough. Secrecy surrounding the court's operations has produced sloppiness and misconduct that would never be tolerated if subjected to the disinfectant of sunlight. The Supreme Court's conferences should be offered for live broadcast. I know, I know—how are the justices supposed to be candid with each other if every word they speak is made public? But, for goodness' sake, these folks have life tenure. What is this protection for, if not to allow them to say what they think without worrying about retribution? If the justices in fact feel a little pressure to think more carefully about what they say in conference, this would be a good result rather than a bad one.

§ *Draft opinions.* The court should release draft opinions for public comment before they are finalized. Why not? Administrative agencies have functioned this way for years. Congress does not usually keep important legislation secret until it becomes law, and when it tries to do so, it is subject to harsh criticism. It is terrifying that the court produces major legal documents in final form without giving interested parties the opportunity to point out errors and suggest revisions.

§ *Reverse oral arguments.* After the draft is made public, the court should conduct reverse oral argument, whereby lawyers for each side can question the justices about the opinion. Why is it only the justices who get to ask the questions? A reverse oral argument, with the advocates posing the hypotheticals and testing limits, might uncover unintended consequences or flabby argumentation. Moreover, forcing the justices to defend their opinions is bound to provide more incentive to think carefully about what they are doing.

Will the Supreme Court adopt these reforms on its own? Don't bet on it. We face a classic chicken-and-egg problem: The justices have power, and their power rests on mystification. We can hardly expect the beneficiaries of this system to dismantle it voluntarily. It does not follow, though, that debate about these proposals is pointless. The necessary first step toward forcing the court to give up its power is to delegitimize the court in the eyes of the public. And the first step in accomplishing that objective is asking why, exactly, the justices are so terrified of reforms that would end the pervasive mystification that encases the court's work. Even considering proposals like these punctures the pomp, pretension, and grandiosity that supports the court's power.

More than that, thinking about these proposals reveals the sheer ridiculousness of the court. Yes, we need to advance reasoned arguments for why this institution is harming the country. But more than just argument is required. The court should be the object of derision, mockery, and contempt. We need to start making fun of the pomposity and pretensions of the justices.

If we can bring ourselves to see through its pomposity and pretensions, perhaps the Supreme Court will lose its power over us. Once it does, the American people can begin the serious work of debating what it would take to establish justice—work that cannot and should not be delegated to an arrogant elite in robes.

John Roberts Gets an F on His Annual Report

Elie Mystal
January 24, 2022

Every December, the chief justice of the Supreme Court of the United States composes a "Year-End Report on the Federal Judiciary." Despite the apparent ambition indicated by its title, it is meant to be boring. It is meant to be anodyne. It is not supposed to be the judicial version of the State of the Union so much as a trite message about how "great" things are going on the bench, usually with some boilerplate stats that show how hard judges are working.

On first read, John Roberts's 2021 review does not disappoint. Opening with a history lesson about the Judicial Conference—an advisory body founded 100 years ago that oversees the administration of the courts—it has all the stylistic markings the media consistently praises Roberts for: It is good-natured, reassuring, and banal to the point of hokey. Never mind that things are far from OK within the judiciary—that the judicial branch has been captured by an army of conservative hacks and the Supreme Court has veered so sharply to the right that even the general public has noticed, dragging its poll numbers to record lows. Roberts's nine-page report concerns itself with none of this. To the untrained eye, it reads as totally innocuous.

I know better, however. Roberts's annual review has all the charms of an old country goose: ordinary and unassuming from a distance, but an irritable, irascible beast that will peck your eyes out if you get too close.

Roberts fashions it as an earnest plea for the "institutional independence" of the judiciary—or "the Judiciary's power to manage its internal affairs." Toward this end, he extols the virtues of the Judicial Conference and the notion that the courts can and should police themselves. But like a child who agrees to be grounded before the full extent of their misdeeds can be revealed, Roberts isn't making this suggestion for some aw-shucks innocent reason. He raises the issue of judicial independence because Congress is finally considering reining in the rampant corruption he himself refuses to stop and punishing the ethics violators he refuses to hold accountable. Of course Roberts wants people to think the judiciary should police itself, because that means judges will not be policed at all.

The issue that seems to have sparked Congress's concern—and Roberts's pushback—is a scandal that rocked the judiciary last year. In September, a *Wall Street Journal* investigation revealed that 131 federal judges improperly heard cases involving companies whose shares the judge or members of the judge's family held. Since that initial article (which covered only cases heard between 2010 and 2018), the *Journal* has reported that 136 judges subsequently informed the parties in 777 lawsuits that they should have recused themselves and that the cases could now be reassigned to other judges or reopened. The corruption uncovered by the *Journal* is a violation of a Watergate-era law that prohibits judges (or members of their family) from owning an interest, however small, in a company that is litigating in front of them. The violations are too numerous to be chalked up as one-off errors and speak to a pervasive disregard for the rules and a culture of impropriety.

Congress recognized this right away. The House held a hearing in October on making judges' financial disclosure forms available to the public (as they are for elected officials), which would help interested parties identify judges who should not be hearing their cases instead of waiting for *The Wall Street Journal* (or the judges themselves) to do it. The Senate Judiciary Committee has proposed modernizing judicial ethics rules and disclosure requirements. And Senator Elizabeth Warren and Representative Pramila Jayapal have expressed interest in legislation that would impose civil sanctions on judges who fail to recuse themselves when they should.

Roberts refuses to brook any of this. In his year-end report, he hits back against the possibility of congressional interference by trying to make people believe the whole problem can be solved with more webinars. "Collectively," he writes, "our ethics training programs need to be more rigorous. That means more classtime, webinars, and consultations. But it also requires greater attention to promoting a culture of compliance, even when busy dockets keep judicial calendars full."

Roberts takes much the same approach to what he calls "inappropriate behavior in the judicial workplace" (which I can only assume refers to sexual harassment, though Roberts declines to name it). Despite consistent reports of sexual harassment and misconduct in the judicial branch, Roberts claims, not for the first time, that "inappropriate workplace conduct is not pervasive within the Judiciary." He then goes on to suggest that expanded guidance and training should resolve the few cases he is willing to admit actually happen. What won't be necessary is congressional interference. "I appreciate that Members of Congress have expressed ongoing concerns on this important matter," he writes, before issuing a final brush-off.

Even the obviously hokey bits have troubling undertones. The report is framed by a discussion of William Howard Taft. Roberts presents Taft as a chief justice who, despite having been president, upheld the principles of judicial independence. But history remembers Taft's time on the court as one that was terrible for workers: The man literally struck down a tax on companies that used child labor. Taft's most famous case is one in which he upheld the president's right to dismiss federal officials without Senate approval, and let's not forget that, as president, Taft all but refused to appoint African Americans as federal officers and dismissed many of those who held office under his predecessor. That's the man Roberts chose to highlight at the end of 2021.

I'd call Roberts's year-end statement "brazen," but he knows that most people in the media aren't aware of Taft's full history or the recusal scandal or the options for ethics reforms. And he knows that even if people did know these things, Democrats in Congress and the White House lack the strength or the vision to rein him and his cohorts in.

Roberts's cries for judicial independence are actually demands that the judiciary be placed above accountability. I guess some branches of government get to be more equal than others.

DEBATE: The Supreme Court Is Broken. How Do We Fix It?

Ryan Doerfler and Elie Mystal
June 6, 2022

Strip Its Power

Ryan Doerfler

With the leak of a draft opinion in *Dobbs v. Jackson Women's Health Organization* formally overruling *Roe v. Wade*, progressives' worst fears about an ever more reactionary Supreme Court appear set to come true.

After decades of chipping away at abortion rights, the court's conservatives—now a rock-solid majority—seem ready to complete that ideological project openly and even triumphantly.

In itself, such a decision would be catastrophic, especially for those who don't have the resources or the personal freedom to travel vast distances to receive basic health care. The draft opinion's unapologetic tone also presages similarly harmful outcomes on issues ranging from contraception to same-sex marriage to immigration to climate change. Indeed, some of these outcomes are already here.

With this parade of horribles about to be realized, progressives are returning with even greater urgency to the question of what to do about the conservative leviathan that is the Supreme Court. As in earlier moments, the temptation is merely to replace that leviathan with a progressive one, packing the court with benevolent justices who will wield the institution's power for good. Real progress, though, requires the beast to be slayed, stripping the court of its authority and returning our society's most pressing and important questions to the democratic arena—where progressive causes, backed by popular movements, stand the best chance.

Considering the history of the federal right to abortion helps to reveal the severe limitations of relying on a juricentric approach to securing fundamental rights. Just four years after the court recognized that right in *Roe*, a nearly identical court declared in *Maher v. Roe* that the state was under no obligation to make abortion economically feasible. Even at the height of its support for reproductive health care, in other words, the court ensured that the right to abortion would be one in name only for millions of women without the financial means.

The Supreme Court's refusal to guarantee meaningful, *positive* rights to US citizens (let alone noncitizens) goes far beyond abortion. Even during the Warren Court era, the historical anomaly to which so many defenders of juristocracy cling, liberal justices failed to extend constitutional protections to America's economic underclass, thereby abandoning an ideal of substantive equality in favor of formal equality.

In addition to failing to provide positive rights, the Supreme Court has, throughout its history, actively impeded Congress from providing such rights through ordinary legislation. Most famously, the court struck down the Civil Rights Act of 1875 in the *Civil Rights Cases*, undercutting Congress's primary effort to guarantee the rights of Black Americans in the aftermath of the Civil War. Much more recently, in a decision hailed by liberal media as "upholding" the Affordable Care Act, the Supreme Court invalidated Congress's expansion of Medicaid, once again depriving poor people of the affirmative right to health care they are so desperately owed.

What this history suggests is that the most plausible path to a meaningful right not only to abortion but also to education or racial equality or climate justice is through federal legislation rather than judicial edict. As history also suggests, such progressive legislation would face eventual judicial resistance—unless Congress were to strip the Supreme Court (and other courts) of its authority to decide on the constitutionality of that law.

By invoking its power under Article III to make "exceptions" to the Supreme Court's jurisdiction over most cases and its total discretion over the existence of "inferior" federal courts, Congress could—and should—insulate legislation like the Women's Health Protection Act from judicial invalidation by including a provision withdrawing from any court the right to consider challenges to the constitutionality of that law. Deploying such jurisdiction-stripping provisions broadly would ensure that the meaning of our Constitution and, more fundamentally, what rights exist within our constitutional order would be determined by (at least somewhat) democratically responsive officials in Congress and the White House, as opposed to democratically insulated philosopher kings.

Removing issues like health care or climate from the courts would have the further advantage of placing responsibility at the feet of elected officials. Rather than speculating about whether some judicial nominee would respect stare decisis, "moderates" in the Senate would have to explain why they do or do not support a right to choose. Similarly, rather than promising, as President Biden has since his election, to enact federal abortion legislation if the Supreme Court overrules *Roe*, he and his party would have to explain why they are not protecting women's reproductive freedom right now.

Finally, although jurisdiction stripping is often characterized as an alternative to court expansion, the two are not mutually exclusive. Given its history, though, merely adding progressive justices to the Supreme Court would yield limited benefits in the short term and leave in place an undemocratic behemoth that would wreak further havoc in the end.

Expand It

Elie Mystal

Let's start with the obvious: I'm in favor of jurisdiction stripping, weather stripping, or stripping while dancing on a pole if that's what it takes to stop the Supreme Court from turning the clock back to 1859. I'm in favor of using any and all nonviolent means available to stop the court's current embrace of bigotry and misogyny. If jurisdiction stripping reminds the court that it is a coequal branch of government and not a judicial clergy, superior to the elected branches, then I'm all for it.

The legal theory behind what has come to be known as jurisdiction stripping is sound. The Supreme Court gave itself the power to declare unconstitutional both laws passed by Congress and orders signed by the president in the 1803 case *Marbury v. Madison.* This power of judicial review was not written into the Constitution nor contemplated during its ratification battle. The Supreme Court invented it, and that means Congress can, in theory, take it away. Congress can pass a law and then exclude that law from judicial review. Congress can, on its own authority, determine what is constitutional and what is not.

This works in theory. My concern is that the Supreme Court will simply ignore attempts to limit its power, and all the time and effort spent convincing politicians that jurisdiction stripping is the answer will leave us exactly where we started: with a high court untroubled by the desires of the American people. Congress will pass a law and include a stipulation saying, "This law is not open for Supreme Court interpretation." Then the Supreme Court will say, "No. In fact, this law passed by Congress is unconstitutional." The Supreme Court can, and likely will, use judicial review to reject congressional attempts to get around judicial review.

What happens next depends a lot on what kind of law Congress attempts to shield from the Supreme Court's interpretation of the Constitution. If it's the kind of law that requires the states to do, or not do, something, the states that agree with Congress will go along with Congress, while the states that agree with the Supreme Court will refuse to follow the "unconstitutional" congressional mandate. Think about jurisdiction stripping in the abortion context: Congress can pass a law that protects a woman's right to choose and prohibits the Supreme Court from reviewing it. The religious fundamentalists will ask the Supreme Court to review the law anyway. It's likely the forced-birth caucus on the Supreme Court will decide that Congress cannot strip its power and then determine, again, that Congress doesn't have the power to protect women's rights. Texas will listen to the court and outlaw abortions; California will listen to Congress and allow them. Nothing will have been solved.

In contrast, the types of laws that are ripe for jurisdiction stripping are those whose implementation the president, as head of the executive branch, has full control over. An environmental regulation on power plants might work. The Supreme Court might say the regulation is unconstitutional, but when armed agents of the federal government come to shut down the delinquent power plant, there's little a Supreme Court decision can do to stop them.

But think about what I'm saying and play the tape all the way to the end. Jurisdiction stripping works only if a president, in command of an army, is willing to defy the Supreme Court's view of itself. That is a dangerous game to play, especially if the goal is to "restore" democracy.

Jurisdiction stripping—the kind that doesn't lead to a military takeover—requires the Supreme Court to willingly relinquish some of its power but does not reform or incentivize the court to relinquish that power. That's why I favor court expansion instead. The problem, to my mind, is not that the Supreme Court is powerful but that we've decided to let conservative extremists wield that power, unchecked, for life.

But imagine this: Instead of starting with jurisdiction stripping, add 20 justices to the court who believe that jurisdiction stripping is constitutional—and then pass legislation not subject to judicial review. Or add 20 justices who believe the Supreme Court should have a code of ethics—and then pass ethics reform. Or give me 20 justices who believe that term limits can be legislated without a constitutional amendment—and then pass term limits legislation. The court needs to be expanded with people who think the court can be restrained, before attempting to restrain the court. You shoot the bear with the tranquilizer dart and then put the tracking collar on it; doing it the wrong way around is how well-meaning folks end up as dinner.

Right now, the law is whatever five Supreme Court justices say it is. The way to fix this is not to pass new laws, as those five people will just ignore laws they don't like anyway. The solution is to flood the court with people who will make better decisions about laws. The Supreme Court must be reformed before it can play well in the sandbox with the other two branches of government.

A Dirty Decision

Elie Mystal
June 23, 2023

On May 25, the Supreme Court released a major ruling that significantly curtails the Environmental Protection Agency's ability to regulate the nation's wetlands under the Clean Water Act. The opinion was handed down while I was waiting for a train, so a very nice lady standing next to me had the misfortune of hearing my first-take rant as I was reading through Justice Samuel Alito's majority opinion. When I finally stopped talking long enough to shove a chicken nugget into my face hole, she said, "The only war we're capable of winning is the one against the environment."

She's right. It's a war being waged by the fossil fuel industry, supported by companies addicted to the profits provided by cheap plastics and given a moral pass by various right-wing Bible thumpers who believe God (instead of gravity) created the earth and gave it to humans. Now, over the objection of most of the American people and various acts of Congress, the Republican-controlled Supreme Court has appointed itself as the shock troops in this war, as the vanguard who take the hopes and dreams of polluters and fashion them into laws.

The court knows exactly where to attack. Last year, in *West Virginia v. EPA*, it eviscerated the Clean Air Act. Now, with *Sackett v. EPA*, the court has come for water. The Clean Air Act and the Clean Water Act are the two foundational laws that the EPA was created to administer. The conservative justices won't overturn these wildly popular acts of Congress outright, so instead they've decided to neuter the EPA's ability to enforce them. The conservative approach to environmental protection is similar to that of locusts: consume every resource and die before having to deal with the consequences of their own destruction.

Sackett v. EPA involves a complicated application of the Clean Water Act. Michael and Chantell Sackett bought a lot near Priest Lake in Idaho, and, well, it was wet. They wanted to fill it with dirt so they could build a home. The EPA prevented its construction, arguing that the Sacketts' property feeds into a tribu tary that feeds into a creek that feeds into Priest Lake. It's long been a knotty legal issue to determine the extent of the EPA's authority over these kinds of situations. The Clean Water Act grants the EPA the authority to regulate the "navigable waters" of the United States, but it defines "navigable waters" as the "waters of the United States," which doesn't really help clarify the issue. (Thanks, Congress.)

Courts have long held that the EPA has the authority to regulate not just large bodies of water like lakes and rivers, but also aquatic ecosystems "adjacent" to those lakes and rivers, which include many of the nation's extensive wetlands. This makes sense, because if you know only two things about water, those should be that it makes things wet—and it flows. If you dump dangerous pollutants into your swamp, it won't be long before they end up in my drinking water. Such is the nature of liquids.

Unfortunately, it would appear that Justice Alito was sick the day they taught fluid dynamics in middle school, and he never went back and did the reading. Writing for the majority in *Sackett*, Alito claims to be unable to distinguish between a wetland or watershed that drains into a lake and a swimming pool or puddle. I'm not exaggerating; the guy literally counters the EPA's experts with a hypothetical about a puddle:

The EPA argues that "waters" is "naturally read to encompass wetlands" because the "presence of water is 'universally regarded as the most basic feature of wetlands.'" ... But that reading proves too much. Consider puddles, which are also defined by the ordinary presence of water even though few would describe them as "waters."

Alito's argument is as deep as one of his puddles. It's true that "waters" is a broad term, but acting like there's no meaningful distinction between a wetland and a puddle shows that Alito is either being intellectually dishonest or is in desperate need of an intervention from Bill Nye.

To resolve this self-imposed ignorance, Alito turns to another word game: parsing the definition of "adjacent." According to Alito, "adjacent" in the context of the Clean Water Act must mean that the wetland shares a "continuous surface connection" with a "navigable" body of water. But Alito's definition is entirely made up. It's made up according to the Supreme Court's own precedents, which, as I said, have previously granted the EPA authority to regulate wetlands that drain into major bodies of water. And it's made up in terms of the common definition of the word "adjacent," which Justice Elena Kagan points out in her opinion. She writes: "In ordinary language, one thing is adjacent to another not only when it is touching, but also when it is nearby."

This brings us back to the actual case at the heart of *Sackett*. As I said, the facts of the Sacketts' particular lot are complicated. Indeed, all nine justices ruled against the EPA and in favor of the Sacketts' plan to fill their lot with dirt. But the justices split 5–4 on how to interpret the Clean Water Act, with four refusing to go along with Alito's fanciful redefinition. Kagan wrote separately, joined by Justices Sonia Sotomayor and Ketanji Brown Jackson, while alleged attempted rapist Brett Kavanaugh also wrote a separate opinion calling Alito out for his lack of understanding of how water filters from a wetland into a larger body of water. I make fun of Kavanaugh and his intelligence a lot in this column, so I must give him credit for understanding how this all works better than his conservative brethren. I guess you can learn a lot from watching how beer spills off a ping-pong table.

This is one of those cases I'm going to have a really hard time explaining to my grandkids when they ask me why the only safe drinking product is Gatorade and all the plants are dying. According to the EPA, Alito's ruling puts over 50 percent of the nation's wetlands at risk from polluters, who will now claim that the water they're dumping into is not covered by the Clean Water Act. The United States is in the midst of a freshwater crisis, with most of what we have left residing underground. How are we to explain to future generations that in 2023, given all we know about our precarious situation, we opened the floodgates to additional water pollution because an old man and four of his ideological friends decided they couldn't tell the difference between groundwater and a swimming pool?

I simply cannot emphasize enough that if you are an environmental activist—or merely a conscious human—you must be loudly in favor of court reform and expansion. All of the protests and legislative campaigns and individual carbon-footprint controls in the world will mean nothing if these unelected conservative justices get to set climate policy for the next 30 years. They are in a war against the environment, and they are winning. Our children will reap the bitter harvest of what the Supreme Court sows now, and when they ask us why we let them do this, they will be unimpressed when we say, "Nine just felt like the right number of justices."

The Biggest Supreme Court Power Grab Since 1803

Elie Mystal
June 28, 2024

In the biggest judicial power grab since 1803, the Supreme Court today overruled *Chevron v. Natural Resources Defense Council*, a 1984 case that instructed the judiciary to defer to the president and the president's experts in executive agencies when determining how best to enforce laws passed by Congress. In so doing, the court gave itself nearly unlimited power over the administrative state and its regulatory agencies.

Now, if you're not a lawyer, that probably sounds bad, but mainly in a technical sense. Regulatory agencies like the Environmental Protection Agency and the Securities and Exchange Commission issue influential but deeply complicated rules, so it makes sense that somebody should have final authority over whether and how to enforce those rules. Since we have already made the disastrous decision to allow the Supreme Court to tell us who gets to be president and what women can be forced to do with their bodies, it might not sound like that big of a leap to also let the court decide how much lead can leak into our drinking water or which predators are allowed to sell mortgages.

The thing is: The US Constitution, flawed though it is, has already answered the question of who gets to decide how to enforce our laws. The Constitution says, quite clearly, that Congress passes laws and the president enforces them. The Supreme Court, constitutionally speaking, has no role in determining whether Congress was right to pass the law, or if the executive branch is right to enforce it, or how presidents should use the authority granted to them by Congress. So, for instance, if Congress passes a Clean Air Act (which it did in in 1963) and the president creates an executive agency to enforce it (which President Richard Nixon did in 1970), then it's really not up to the Supreme Court to say, "Well, actually, 'clean air' doesn't mean what the EPA thinks it means."

For an unelected panel of judges to come in, above the agencies, and tell them how the president is allowed to enforce laws is a perversion of the constitutional order and separation of powers—and a repudiation of democracy itself.

But repudiating democracy to expand its own power is exactly what the Supreme Court did today in its ruling in *Loper Bright Enterprises v. Raimondo*, which overturned *Chevron*. In a 6-3 decision, which split exactly along party lines, Chief Justice John Roberts ruled that the courts—and, more particularly, his court and the people who have bought and paid for the justices on it—are the sole arbiters of which laws can be enforced and what enforcement of those laws must look like. Roberts ruled that courts, and only courts, are allowed to figure out what Congress meant to do and impose those interpretations on the rest of society. He wrote that "agencies have no special competence in resolving statutory ambiguities. Courts do."

That is a naked power grab that places the court ahead of literal experts chosen by the president, who is the one elected official we all get to vote for. Who do you think has a "special competence" in resolving what the word "clean" means in the context of the "Clean Water" or "Clean Air" act—experts at the EPA or justices on Harlan Crow's yacht? Who do you think has a special competence to resolve what "safe" working conditions require—experts at the Occupational Safety and Health Administration or justices who have never worked as much as a day at a job that requires them to be outside? Who do you think has a special competence to resolve what "equality" means under the Civil Rights Act for women in workplaces—experts at the Equal Employment Opportunity Commission or justices who have been accused of attempted rape?

Even if you do think, somehow, that judges are best positioned to determine how to enforce the laws passed by Congress, who in the hell gave them the power to do so? Not the Constitution. When Congress and the president talk about how to do the work of the people, and the Supreme Court butts in, the official constitutional response to the court is, "I don't remember asking you a goddamn thing."

Despite the actual structure of the Constitution and all of its amendments, the Supreme Court, as an institution, has fought to exceed the limits of its constitutional power from the very beginning. Its ruling in *Loper Bright* is only its latest and most brazen move to set itself up as the ultimate and final authority in the nation. As I said, the appropriate historical context for its ruling today is not 1984 and its *Chevron* decision but its 1803 ruling in *Marbury v. Madison*. It was then, back when the country was still in its swaddling blankets, that the Supreme Court declared itself the sole interpreter of the Constitution. The word "unconstitutional" appears nowhere in the Constitution, and the power to decide what is or is not constitutional was not given to the court in the Constitution or by any of the amendments. The court decided for itself that it had the power to revoke acts of Congress and declare actions by the president "unconstitutional," and the elected branches went along with it.

Even now, this is perplexing. The court has no enforcement power of its own, so there's no inherent reason either the president or Congress has to defer to its demands, other than by convention and tradition. Yet the normal thing is for the court to issue a ruling, after which the elected branches are expected to do all the work of bending themselves to the court's will. Sometimes, presidents just ignore the court (as Andrew Jackson, Abraham Lincoln, and Franklin Delano Roosevelt did) and wait for the court to figure out that nobody cares. Other times, the legislature will ignore the court, or drag its feet before implementing the court's rules (as Southern state legislatures did after *Brown v. Board of Education*, essentially refusing to desegregate until John F. Kennedy sent federal troops down to make them do it). But most of the time, the elected branches will largely do what the court tells it to do, even though nobody elected the court, and the Constitution doesn't give the court the power to make the rules.

Sometimes, however, there will be a flash point when the Supreme Court grabs as much power as it can stuff in its pockets and dares anyone to stop them. That's what happened in *Marbury v. Madison*, and that's also what happened in 2000, after the court's ruling in *Bush v. Gore*. In that case, the Supreme Court picked the president instead of letting Florida recount the votes of its people.

As in *Marbury*, the officials who were constitutionally empowered by the people just let the court have its way. Bill Clinton, the actual president at the time, accepted that the court could decide which votes were counted. Jeb Bush, who was the governor of Florida, accepted that the Supreme Court could pick his brother for president. George W. Bush gleefully accepted that the court could install him as president (even though Bush may have actually won the recount in Florida, and thus could have won the presidential election legitimately under a normal democratic process). And Al Gore conceded defeat to the Supreme Court.

Twenty-four years later, the ruling in *Loper Bright* effectively completes the suite of powers the Supreme Court has given itself to lord over everybody else. The court can now: veto acts of Congress as unconstitutional, decide who gets to be president, and decide what the president is allowed to do while in office.

I do not believe the court would have made the jump from picking the president to assuming the role and powers constitutionally given to the presidency if the conservative justices weren't already sure that the people were too weak to stop them. But the conservatives were sure they could get away with today's ruling because they already got away with a different case two years ago: *Dobbs v. Jackson Women's Health Organization*. *Dobbs* is critical because *Dobbs* involved the court taking away a popular, fundamental right for the first time in American history. No other case, not *Marbury v. Madison*, not *Bush v. Gore*, involved unelected, lifetime appointees revoking by fiat a right previously enjoyed by the American people.

And you know what happened to the Supreme Court after *Dobbs*? Nothing. Sure, a lot of people were and remained pissed. And yes, some political candidates have paid an electoral price for the court's extremist ruling. But neither the people nor their elected representatives have done one solitary thing to stop the court, reform it, or take away its power. The court's "approval rating" has gone down, but its budget has remained unchanged, and its power has remained unchecked.

Not one justice has even been hauled in front of Congress to be *questioned* about the *Dobbs* ruling. (The fourth estate, the media, has also wholly failed to hold the court accountable for its actions.). Astute court watchers will note that barricades went up around the court in 2022 because the court anticipated a reaction to its revocation of reproductive rights—but no reaction happened. Today, there was no security presence as the court blithely gave itself ultimate authority over all laws and regulations. The court knows that the people are too addled and distracted to even raise a sustained protest against its rulings.

To call ourselves a "democracy" after today is a sick joke. We are not a democracy. We are a nation that is allowed to make suggestions to our nine rulers on the Supreme Court, but those rulers are the ones who get to decide which suggestions they accept and which ones they ignore. It is the *opposite* of the structure outlined in the Constitution—the one where the people, through their elected representatives, make the rules while the unelected court merely addresses conflicts between the two elected branches or between the elected federal officials and elected state officials.

Frankly, we don't deserve democracy. We haven't earned it. We haven't fought to protect it, and what little we inherited from the heroic efforts of the civil rights generation we've pissed away on presidential "debates" and political candidates we'd like to have a beer with. The Supreme Court dominates our elected branches of government because our political leaders lack the strength to do otherwise. We deserve no better than the yoke the court has fashioned for us, because *we* are the ones putting it on.

I wish I had better news for you. I wish I could say, "We just have to clap very hard in the next election and Tinkerbell will live and restore *Roe v. Wade*." But this isn't a fairy tale. There is literally nothing that can be done to restore the rights the Supreme Court has taken away, or restore the power the Constitution gives to the people, other than reforming the Supreme Court and flooding it with justices who do not think they are kings. Court expansion is *the only way* to stop the Supreme Court. But to expand the court we have to elect Democrats, many of whom are also against court expansion. Then we have to push those Democrats to get rid of the filibuster, which many of them don't want to do. Then we have to get Democrats to use their power. Then we have to get the Democratic president to put the right kinds of justices on the court. And we have to do it all over the unified objection of the Republican Party, the Christian right, the fossil fuel industry, the financial services industry, your racist uncle who watches Fox News, and Ice Cube.

That's ... probably not going to happen. And the Supreme Court knows it. They're counting on it. They're about to go on a summer-long vacation and leave us to have our reality-television show *Democracy* where the viewers place their votes but the producers pick the winners. When they come back in the fall, fattened by the "gratuities" they just declared it was legal for them to take, they'll let us know who is allowed to be president again—and then get back to work taking away more of our rights.

We Rejected Monarchy in 1776.
The Supreme Court Just Brought It Back.

John Nichols
July 4, 2024

"There are no kings in America," declared President Biden after the United States Supreme Court reinterpreted the Constitution to afford monarchical immunity powers to American presidents.

Biden's point was true enough, at least for the moment. But there have been kings in this land before. A lot of them. From 1607 to 1783, the eastern seaboard of the North American continent was governed by King James I, King Charles I, King Charles II, King James II, King William III, Queen Mary II, Queen Anne, King George I, King George II, and, finally, King George III, who like many of his predecessors, was a raging madman.

The greatest contribution to the progress of humanity made by the colonialists forging the United States was their revolt against King George III and the brutal lie that imagined a "divine right of kings." Theirs was an Enlightenment-inspired revolution whose finest champion, Thomas Paine, described as "the cause of all mankind."

"The sun never shined on a cause of greater worth," wrote Paine in *Common Sense*, his revolutionary call to arms. "'Tis not the affair of a city, a county, a province, or a kingdom, but of a continent—of at least one eighth part of the habitable globe. 'Tis not the concern of a day, a year, or an age; posterity are virtually involved in the contest, and will be more or less affected, even to the end of time, by the proceedings now."

With the American Revolution against monarchy and empire, argued Paine, "a new era for politics is struck; a new method of thinking hath arisen."

To this day, we celebrate that new thinking on July 4, as the moment when, again borrowing Paine's language, the choice was made "to begin the world over again."

After this revolution succeeded, the founders of what would come to be known as the American experiment wrote a Constitution that contained some fundamentally flawed ideas— from the grotesque calculus that accepted human bondage to the establishment of an Electoral College that is subverting our democracy to this very day. Yet the founders got one thing very right. Because of their bitter experience with monarchy, they established a system of checks and balances that was designed to guard at every turn against monarchical excess.

The Congress, particularly the elected House of Representatives, was to be supreme. As House Judiciary Committee member Jamie Raskin, the Maryland Democrat who is the House's great constitutional scholar, says,

> We are not a coequal branch. We are the first among equals. We are in Article 1 of the Constitution. We are the representatives of the people. When you look at the powers of Congress,

they are comprehensive and abundant. The president's core job is to take care that the laws are faithfully executed, not thwarted and circumvented, much less violated.

To check and balance such violations, the Congress was given the power of the purse, as well the ultimate power to impeach and remove presidents and errant executives—a power it has failed, repeatedly, to embrace with the energy and determination that was intended by the founders or required by the moment.

But legislative oversight was not the only method of checking presidential power that was outlined in the Constitution. The courts were given their own authority to constrain presidents and their administrations.

Even with those constitutional guardrails, however, the wisest founders worried. It is reported that Benjamin Franklin, following the signing of the Constitution in September of 1787, was asked by Elizabeth Willing Powel, "Well, Doctor, what have we got, a republic or a monarchy?"

Franklin famously responded, "A republic, if you can keep it."

The United States Senate failed to *keep it* in 2021, when Republicans who—after Trump had been impeached by a bipartisan majority in the House—cast a sufficient number of votes to block the conviction of Trump for his efforts to overturn the results of the 2020 election. At the time, Senate minority leader Mitch McConnell (R-KY) justified this dereliction of duty by claiming, "The Constitution gives us a particular role. This body is not invited to act as the nation's overarching moral tribunal." Instead, McConnell suggested, "We have a criminal justice system in this country. We have civil litigation. And former presidents are not immune from being held accountable by either one."

But on July 1, 2024, 72 hours before Americans would celebrate the 248th anniversary of the Declaration of Independence, a 6-3 majority of Republican-appointed conservative legal activists on the Supreme Court determined — at the behest of Donald Trump — that presidents *and* former presidents have broad immunity from criminal prosecution for "official acts" while in office. Chief Justice John Roberts spelled it out when he announced that "the nature of presidential power entitles a former president to absolute immunity from criminal prosecution for actions within his conclusive and preclusive constitutional authority."

While Americans were looking up the definition of "preclusive," Justice Sonia Sotomayor explained that, with its decision in the immunity case, the court's majority "makes a mockery of the principle, foundational to our Constitution and system of government, that no man is above the law."

Then, Justice Sotomayor pointed to the fundamental reality that extends from the court's decision: "In every use of official power, the President is now a king above the law."

Sotomayor concluded her response to the court's decision by announcing: "With fear for our democracy, I dissent."

Benjamin Franklin and his compatriots gave us a republic, if we could keep it. As of now, we are not keeping it. This is the truth that should be acknowledged on July 4, 2024. And it is the threat that should be addressed on November 5, 2024.

This is, to put it mildly, a politically turbulent moment, but one truth is self-evident: Unless Americans elect a president who respects the Constitution's written constraints on his power— as opposed to the reinterpreted fantasy of the current Supreme Court—the monarchical threat will be realized. And even if that threat is averted this fall, the work of the republic will be incomplete. Until a constitutionally inclined president and an allied Senate move to expand the membership of the high court so that a new majority can undo the damage done on July 1, 2024, this country's revolutionary promise will remain in a new variation on the peril that led Thomas Paine to observe, "These are the times that try men's souls."

List of Contributors

Paul Y. Anderson was a widely celebrated muckraking journalist who helped expose the Teapot Dome scandal. He began writing a regular column for *The Nation* in 1929 until his death by suicide in 1938, when editor Freda Kirchwey celebrated him as "a high-hearted fighter, sometimes truculent and provocative, always courageous."

Nan Aron is the founder and former president of Alliance for Justice, a progressive advocacy organization.

Kyle C. Barry is director of the State Law Research Initiative, a legal advocacy organization. He has also served as senior policy counsel at the NAACP Legal Defense and Educational Fund and as the director of justice programs at Alliance for Justice.

Ari Berman is a correspondent for *Mother Jones* and a reporting fellow at Type Media Center. He is the author, most recently, of *Minority Rule: The Right-Wing Attack on the Will of the People—and the Fight to Resist It* (2024).

Maxwell Brandwen was a lawyer for the Amalgamated Clothing Workers of America.

Jedediah Britton-Purdy is a professor of law at Duke University and the author of books including *This Land Is Our Land: The Struggle for a New Commonwealth* (2019) and *Two Cheers* *for Politics: Why Democracy Is Scary, Flawed, and Our Best Hope* (2022).

Vincent Bugliosi was a prosecutor, most famous for investigating Charles Manson and his accomplices, and the author of several books. His article for *The Nation* about *Bush v. Gore* was later expanded into a book, *The Betrayal of America* (2001).

Raymond Leslie Buell was a social scientist and researcher who received his Ph.D. from Princeton University in 1922, the year he wrote about the Supreme Court for *The Nation*. He later led the Foreign Policy Association, wrote books about international relations, and advised magazine publisher Henry Luce.

James D. Carroll was a lawyer and longtime professor at the Maxwell School of Citizenship and Public Affairs at Syracuse University.

Morris R. Cohen, born in Minsk, was an influential legal scholar, professor of philosophy at the City University of New York, and a major influence on several generations of students, best known for his pragmatist work, *Reason and Nature* (1931).

David Cole is *The Nation*'s legal affairs correspondent, national legal director of the American Civil Liberties Union, and professor of constitutional law, national security, and criminal justice at Georgetown University Law Center. He first contributed to *The Nation* in 1989.

Earl B. Dickerson was a World War I veteran, civil-rights lawyer, and leader in the NAACP who successfully argued a case related to racial housing discrimination before the Supreme

Court—*Hansberry v. Lee* (1940). In 1941, Franklin Roosevelt appointed Dickerson to the Fair Employment Practices Committee.

Ryan Doerfler is a professor at Harvard Law School and the author of numerous articles in law journals as well as *Dissent, Jacobin*, the *New York Times*, and the *Washington Post*.

Isidor Feinstein—he changed his name to I.F. Stone the year this article was published—was one of the most influential investigative journalists of the twentieth century. He was a frequent contributor to *The Nation*—eventually its Washington editor—before starting his own *I.F. Stone's Weekly*, which he published from 1953 to 1971.

Michael Klarman teaches constitutional law and history at Harvard University. He is the author of *The Framers' Coup: The Making of the United States Constitution* (2016), and other books.

Sanford Levinson has taught constitutional law at the University of Texas at Austin since 1980. He is the author of numerous books, including *Constitutional Faith* (1988), *An Argument Open to All: Reading the Federalist in the 21st Century* (2015), and, with Cynthia Levinson, *Fault Lines in the Constitution: The Framers, Their Fights, and the Flaws that Affect Us Today* (2017).

K.N. Llewellyn was an influential legal scholar and a leading proponent of the legal realist school in the United States. He taught at Columbia University before moving to the University of Chicago in 1951.

Arthur S. Miller was a professor of constitutional law at Georgetown University and the author or editor of fifteen books, including *The Supreme Court and American Capitalism* (1968).

Elie Mystal is *The Nation*'s justice correspondent and host of the podcast "Contempt of Court." He is the author of *Allow Me to Retort: A Black Guy's Guide to the Constitution* (2022).

John Nichols is a national affairs correspondent for *The Nation*, to which he has contributed since 1994. His most recent book, co-written with Senator Bernie Sanders, is *It's OK To Be Angry About Capitalism* (2024).

Eli Noam is a professor of economics, public policy, and business responsibility at Columbia University.

Katha Pollitt is a poet, essayist, and critic who has written for *The Nation* since 1975. She is the author of, among other books, *Pro: Reclaiming Abortion Rights* (2014).

Jamie Raskin has represented Maryland's 8th Congressional District in the House of Representatives since 2017. He previously taught constitutional law at American University. He is the author of *Overruling Democracy: The Supreme Court Versus the American People* (2003), among other works.

Robert Sherrill was a frequent contributor to *The Nation* from 1964 to 1982, and for many years its Washington correspondent. Listed on Richard Nixon's enemies list, Sherrill was denied a White House press pass, prompting the ACLU to successfully sue on his behalf. Still, Sherrill declined to apply for one. "I didn't want to be in the White House," he said. "I had been in Washington long enough to realize that was the last place to waste your time sitting around."

Bruce Shapiro is executive director of the Dart Center for Journalism and Trauma at Columbia University and a contributing editor to *The Nation*.

Louis Michael Seidman is a professor of constitutional law at Georgetown University Law Center and the author of *On Constitutional Disobedience* (2013), among other works.

Herman Schwartz is a professor of law emeritus at American University's Washington College of Law and a frequent contributor to *The Nation* on legal and judicial issues from 1979 to 2017.

Nadine Strossen, a New York Law School professor and former president of the American Civil Liberties Union, is the author of *HATE: Why We Should Resist It With Free Speech, Not Censorship* (Oxford University Press 2018).

Mark Tushnet is a professor of constitutional law at Harvard Law School and the author of numerous books, including *Taking Back the Constitution: Activist Judges and the Next Age of American Law* (2020).

Charles Warren was a Boston lawyer and Harvard historian who published a Pulitzer Prize-winning history of the Supreme Court in 1922. An advocate of immigration restriction and opponent of women's suffrage, he helped draft the Espionage Act of 1917. This was the only article he wrote for *The Nation*.

Fredric Wertham was a German-American psychologist whose research on the effects of racial segregation was cited by the Court in *Brown v. Board of Education* (1954). He also famously advocated against the depiction of violence and sexuality in comic books.

Patricia J. Williams is a professor of law at Northeastern University and the author of *The Alchemy of Race and Rights: Diary of a Law Professor* (1991), as well as many other books. She contributed to *The Nation* from 1991 to 2022.

Photo by Eva Deitch

Richard Kreitner is a contributing writer to *The Nation* and the author of *Break It Up: Secession, Division, and the Secret History of America's Imperfect Union* (2020) and *Fear No Pharaoh: American Jews, the Civil War, and the Fight to End Slavery* (2025).